"I CRIED, HE ANSWERED"

A Faithful Record of Remarkable Answers to Prayer

Compiled and Edited by
HENRY W. ADAMS, NORMAN H. CAMP,
WILLIAM NORTON and F. A. STEVEN

With Introduction by
CHARLES GALLAUDET TRUMBULL

Schmul Publishers

Rare Reprint Specialists

Salem, Ohio 44460

PUBLISHERS' ANNOUNCEMENT

For some time the publishers have felt the need of a fresh book of testimonies to answered prayer. In order to meet this need, they arranged for its compilation by a representative Editorial Committee, seeking to cover a wide range of common, or everyday objects, as told by living witnesses, both young and old, and of various walks of life.

The work of the Committee finds expression in this volume. To the many friends who have made this compilation possible through hearty co-operation, the Committee and the Publishers owe a large debt of gratitude.

For several reasons, it was thought best not to publish the names of the contributors to the book, but the authorship of the contributors comprising the volume can be authenticated, and when requested, for good reason shown, the publishers will furnish the names and addresses of such contributors as may be designated.

The "Subject Index" on pages 126 and 127 will assist in guiding to definite instances of answered prayer which may inspire the reader to lay hold of God for a similar blessing.

Copyright, 1918
by
THE BIBLE INSTITUTE COLPORTAGE ASSOCIATION
of Chicago

Printed by
Old Paths Tract Society
Shoals, Indiana 47581

"ASK"

Let us come in full assurance,
  We whose hearts are purified
By the precious blood of Jesus
  And in whom His words abide;
Great things let us ask, undoubting,
  Through our faith in Him made bold;
He is faithful that has promised,—
  He will nothing good withhold!

There is One whose love unbounded
  Gave His Son that we might live;
How shall He not with Him, also,
  All things else as "freely give"?
"Thou shalt call, and *I will answer,*"
  Such th' assurance giv'n of old;
And He's faithful that has promised,—
  He will nothing good withhold!

Be ye anxious, then, in nothing;
  Ask of God, through His dear Son;
Every one that asks, receiveth,
  "What ye will—it shall be done."
Fear not, faint not, doubt not, cease not,
  Pray through hindrances untold;
He is faithful that has promised,—
  He will nothing good withhold!

—Mabel Johnston Camp.

INTRODUCTION

We never have to choose between service and prayer. We never have to choose between working or praying. For prayer is service; prayer is work of the most efficient kind that any human being can render. The commonly used expression, "prayer and service," often on the lips of sincere Christians, is a mistaken one. It implies that prayer is one thing and service another, whereas those serve best who pray, and they serve *while they are praying.*

For prayer, as has well been said, "releases the energies of God." Prayer is asking God to do what we cannot do.

Every true prayer originates with God.

Every true prayer is brought from the heart of God by the Holy Spirit to the heart of man.

Every true prayer, thus originated by God and conveyed to the heart of man, when offered in the only true way in the name of Jesus, is carried back to God by the Holy Spirit.

And every true prayer finds its efficiency in the resulting work which God Himself accomplishes in answer.

We all have the marvelous privilege of permitting *or preventing* this working of the omnipotence of God.

Here is a book that is a mighty challenge and invitation to pray. It is like a note-book of the results of laboratory experiments. If principles of the scientific world work out exactly as scientific law says they will, so do principles in God's spiritual world. This book proves it. The experience of every praying Christian proves it. Best of all, God's Word declares it; therefore, we can and must believe it even before it has been proved for us individually. For God's Word is better than any proof or evidence of God's Word.

Introduction

Do we really believe God? Do we believe Him to the uttermost? If so, we shall pray. And praying, we shall cultivate the prayer life. You cannot cultivate a garden without gardening. You cannot cultivate the prayer-life without praying. Reading this book will not do it. Even studying the Word of God will not do it, though that ought to be done. The real cultivating will come in real praying. And we can start that, if we have not hitherto been faithful, even before reading this book.

So many Christians are too busy to pray. Satan intends that they shall be. In "A Call to Prayer," a powerful British writer, explaining Satan's dread of prayer, says: "He knows he cannot frighten saints with hideous features, or overcome them by coarse enticements. He stands at the portal of prayer as an 'angel of light.' He does not attack, he diverts. The church that lacks prayer is usually *full of good works*. Activities are multiplied that devotion and meditation may be ousted, and organizations are increased that prayer may have no chance. Souls may be lost in good works, as surely as in evil ways. The one concern of the devil is to keep the saints from prayer. He fears nothing from prayerless studies, prayerless work, prayerless religion. He laughs at our toil, mocks at our wisdom, but *trembles when we pray.*"

Over against this subtle, diabolical opposition to prayer stands the glorious fact that when we pray according to God's will in faith in the name of Jesus, creative omnipotence springs forward to answer.

When we remember that it was through Christ that every act of creation in the universe has always been wrought, it is not strange that nothing can prevent the answers to prayer when rightly offered in the name of that Creator. Thus it was that Jesus could say (John 15:7) that the abiding Christian, in whom His words abide, may ask whatsoever he will and it shall be *created* unto him. The word "done" in that verse, "and it shall be done unto you," is the Greek word *ginomai,* meaning, to come into existence, receive being, be made. It is the same word as in John 1:3, "All things were *made* through him"; the

Introduction

same word as in the passage, "Command that these stones *become* bread" (Matt. 4:3); and, "The water now *become* wine" (John 2:9, R. V.).

So, as some one has truly said, Jesus urges us to ask for whatever we need, in His name, and He pledges us that He will answer even if, to do so, He needs to "create into being" the thing that we need.

It is worth while to pray: worth while to those for whom we pray; worth while to us; but best of all, worth while to God.

CHARLES GALLAUDET TRUMBULL.

CONTENTS

CHAPTER		PAGE
I.	Prayer for the Recovery of the Sick	11
II.	Prayer for Financial Aid	24
III.	Prayer for Deliverance in Time of Danger	43
IV.	Prayer for Guidance	54
V.	Prayer for the Conversion of Individuals	73
VI.	Prayer for Revivals	91
VII.	Prayer for Various Objects	98
VIII.	Prayer in Relation to Missions and Missionaries	108

[For "Subject Index," see pages 126 and 127]

"I Cried, He Answered"

CHAPTER I.

PRAYER FOR THE RECOVERY OF THE SICK.

Given Up to Die.

My older boy had been given up to die. The doctor said that he would never regain consciousness. I was sent for. The boy was lying in a stupor on his grandmother's lap, looking like a corpse. I prayed earnestly for God to spare the child's life, I arose from my knees and told my wife that she need not worry, for God had assured me that He would heal the boy. He awoke quite bright in the morning and had no recurrence of his trouble and today stands five feet, nine inches tall—a picture of health.   E. L. B.

Lunacy Cured.

In a revival an evangelist preached a week on the subject, "Are the days of miracles past?" During the week he called for a day of fasting and prayer. During the day the revivalist was asked to step into a side room. Several women gathered round him, and weeping said that they were convinced and had banded themselves together to pray for a sister in the lunatic asylum who was pronounced hopeless by the physicians, that the family and church sorely needed her, and that they would never cease praying until she was healed. That very week she was restored to her right mind. The physician said it was entirely unaccountable to him.   T. T. M.

Healed of an "Incurable" Internal Disorder.

My aunt was critically ill. She had been taken to one of the leading hospitals in Chicago. Prominent physicians were baffled with her condition and, after several months, said they could do nothing farther. There was an internal disorder which could not be diagnosed. She was a very earnest Christian, and when pronounced incurable, and removed to her home as such, she commended her case to the Lord, and sought His healing power. What man could not do, in that he is weak, God did, and my aunt, who was then in middle life, was cured almost as quickly as I can write this message of praise and testimony, and lived on to a ripe old age. She never had a recurrence of the disorder.

P. W. S.

Hearing Restored.

While a pastor in Illinois, one day a sharp noise, almost like the snap of a small revolver, startled me and I found that the drum of my left ear had broken. I was sent by Dr. Boynton to one of the best ear specialists in Chicago, who would give me no hopes, saying that a puncture of that size seldom healed. I made him ten visits, and he said the ear was no better except in general appearance. I had told Dr. Boynton that I wanted God to heal me and asked him to pray for me. I asked the prayers of others also. I prayed daily for several weeks for healing. After the tenth visit to the doctor I went to my room in the Moody Bible Institute and had an especially earnest time in prayer. I retired, resting my case assuringly with God. When I awoke next morning my hearing was entirely restored, seeming more acute than before.

E. L. B.

Public Prayer for a Sick Son.

Doctor Brown declares that he has realized large dividends on his investments in Christ through prayer. Recently word came to him that his son, who lives in a distant state, had been well nigh fatally injured in an accident. Several days would be required to reach the bedside of the injured man and the mother started on the journey. Telegraph messages came daily to the father reporting the serious condition of the son. On prayer meeting night he was in his place at the church, and some friends noted his sorrow-lined face, found out the cause, and asked that they might be permitted to publicly pray for the son. This fellowship proved to be a great comfort to the father, as the boy, his doctor and nurse were remembered at the throne of grace. Almost immediately the telegraphic bulletins showed improvement.

A. E. M.

Prayer of Faith Offered 500 Miles Away Effectual.

I got a telegram that my sister, five hundred miles away, was to undergo an operation that afternoon, and that there was but one chance in a hundred that she would survive. I prayed for three hours and got the assurance that she would live. Next morning I was called over long-distance telephone, and the operator said it was a death-message. I refused to believe it. They were calling for me to come on next train, saying that she was better and wanted to see me. My mother wrote me a letter which I got next day, saying that at 5:30 p. m., the day I prayed, sister opened her eyes and said: "Mother, Buddy prayed for me and God told him I might get well." She went immediately into a state of coma, and the physician said she had spoken in the delirium of death. She seemed to be dying all night, but at 6 a. m., next morning she looked up, and asked for water; then said: "Send for Buddy; he prayed for me and I am going to get well." That was nine years ago and she is living today.

L. E. F.

Optic Nerves Restored.

It was while at the Bible Institute (Chicago) in 1898 that I had serious trouble with the optic nerve, so that I was unable to study or read more than perhaps five minutes continuously. The retina of the eyes became so exceedingly sensitive that even the light was painful.

I was excused from all class work, and for the first time in my life began to think of calling upon God for divine healing. I had heard Dr. R. A. Torrey speak on this subject in the class room; so I went to him and asked if he thought God would be pleased to intervene in my case. Dr. Torrey said he was sure that if I would take my stand on the promise in James 5: 14-16, God would heal me.

Accordingly we arranged that at Dr. Torrey's home he would anoint me that day at noon. At the appointed hour, together with Mrs. Curtis, we went to the home of our friend. After the anointing and prayer, I went directly to my study and took up all my class work.

N. R. C.

Healed of a Painful Affliction.

In the year 1916 I learned that, according to Galatians 2:20, it is our privilege to work and pray and live by "the faith of the Son of God." I immediately proceeded to make a practical use of this new-found truth.

While visiting a noble Christian woman of advanced age I was asked to pray that she might be healed of an affliction that had caused her much suffering. She had not been able to sleep for a number of nights. Her faith was being tested most severely. Many years before she had been healed in answer to prayer, but now she was unable to prevail with God and her mind was considerably perplexed. I gave her some instruction on taking Christ for our faith and she began to grasp this precious truth. We prayed and God answered. A few weeks later I received a letter from her daughter telling the good news that her mother had been restored to a normal physical condition. Jesus Christ is made unto us wisdom and righteousness and sanctification and redemption, that is, *deliverance* (1 Cor. 1:30).

C. G. U.

A Child's Life Spared.

When our first-born child was four months old he had gained only about one pound in weight, and looked almost like a skeleton. Many in the community thought he would not live, and the doctor's wife wished me to prepare my wife for the worst by instructing me to tell her not to set her hopes on raising the baby. But we believed in taking everything to God in prayer, and we did not give up hope. Soon after he began to improve and continued to grow stronger until he was nearly a year old, when he was laid low with a severe attack of pneumonia. Looking from the human standpoint, there seemed to be little hope of his recovery. However my wife and I believed that with God nothing was impossible and we brought the case before Him in prayer. He graciously spared the life of our little boy, and today he is healthy and strong (now almost five years old). In times of extremity we know that God does not fail those who put their trust in Him.

E. L. B.

Healed After the Physicians Had Given Up.

Some ten years ago my physician had given up hope of my recovery, as I had been practically an invalid for ten years. Then I said, "Lord, I am ready to come, but if you will heal and keep me well, I will work for you." I had not fully surrendered to Him before. The Lord not only healed me, but I have not spent two weeks in bed since.

Shortly after this I heard Dr. Gray, Dean of the Moody Bible Institute of Chicago, and felt the need of more funds to work with, and the Lord heard me for this, and where I had five or ten dollars per month I now have from fifty to seventy. I prayed also that I might know His Word, and I now teach from two to five Bible classes each week.

I was once praying for money to buy Bibles for a class, and while praying the door bell rang and a gentleman gave me ten dollars.

Before I learned the secret of power in prayer I was much hindered by poor health and discouraged by the enemy.

Mrs. J. H. P.

In an Hour of Failing Strength.

After a long period of constant speaking, twice a day, I began to feel my nerve force slipping away. Each day there was a perceptible increase of nervous exhaustion, and I was almost confident after each service that I should be compelled to give up all engagements. But "this poor man cried, and the Lord heard him." One afternoon, when I felt worse than ever, and was doubtful whether I should get through with the service, instead of going to pieces I found myself completely rested and refreshed when the meeting was over. Then I learned that special prayer had been offered for me that morning by the friends who had invited me to the place.

A month later I lunched with a friend in St. Louis, an elect lady to whom God has given the ministry of prayer. At the table she told me of a prayer meeting in Detroit at which special prayer had been offered for me and of the great blessing that had been given. I inquired about the time of the meeting and found that it was the very hour in which I was so lifted up in Philadelphia.

G. E. G.

A Child's Prayer Is Effectual.

My earliest recollection of answered prayer was when I was about five years old. My younger sister had typhoid fever, the doctor said, and I remember he looked very serious, and that my mother was crying. Whispered conversations and a word I could catch from one and another impressed me that there was danger.

Very well do I remember going alone, and asking directly for what I wanted. The definiteness of that prayer remains clear in my memory, although forty years have passed since then.

There was no preface, or working up to the point of asking, I simply said: "O Jesus, please make my sister well." I expected an answer and to receive what was asked. It was no surprise to me that she grew better, has fully recovered, and is living today. I told no one of what I had done, either at the time or afterwards. It seemed to me it was a private matter between Jesus and myself. Of course, I now know that such praying is in harmony with His revealed will (Matt. 6:6).

R. U. Y. F.

Delivered from Pneumonia.

I was pastor of a village church. A woman of our congregation was apparently near death with pneumonia. She had several small children, and her husband was not a professor of religion. The entire community was deeply interested, and especially the church. The mid-week prayer service was devoted entirely to prayer for her. People who were not able to attend the service prayed for her at home. Many spent the entire evening on their knees in prayer. We prayed that she might be spared for the sake of her children and her husband, and that whether it were the will of God to spare her life or not her husband might be led to Him through this crisis. The doctor and nurse were praying Christians, and were uniting with the rest of us as they worked and watched with her. To their trained vision every indication pointed to death, and they were ready to say that it was God's will to take her away. Suddenly, without reason that the doctor could account for, she began to breathe differently and every symptom improved. She had a satisfactory convalescence, and is today a happy, active Christian. The husband has since been led to Christ, and now exerts the influence of a strong life to the advancement of the kingdom. The children are already giving promise of lives of piety and usefulness.

W. G. O.

Infant Snatched from Death's Door.

We had been married for some years. Our heart's desire was for a child of our own. With hearts full of joy and gratitude we finally welcomed a son. He was born in one of Chicago's hospitals, and a few days after his birth became very ill. The physicians of the institution, as well as our family doctor, quietly and sympathetically conveyed to me their despair, our own doctor saying significantly, "We have done all human effort and medical skill can do. We fear the boy cannot live. Prepare for the worst, but keep the sad news from the child's mother."

Was God mocking us? Were we not active and faithful Christians? Had we not prayed for this child? Could God take him from us? With these and many other questions, a group of four or five Christians laid the matter before God, arguing our case. This prayer group prayed between nine and ten at night. Early the next morning the nurse at the hospital met me in the long passage way and said, smilingly, "Oh! the most remarkable change came over your boy last night about 9:30. His temperature went down; he slept very well through the night, and this morning we know he will live." He had a strenuous struggle with death, but today he is a stalwart, bright, Christian youth, whom we expect later to "preach the Gospel."

E. L. R.

An Operation Averted.

In the winter of 1913 I was holding a series of evangelistic meetings in Calumet, Mich. My family lived in our home in Pontiac, same state. A letter came from my wife saying that our little daughter Ruth was very sick, and this was followed by a telegram carrying the news that three doctors had been in consultation and had decided to perform a serious operation on a date a few days hence. I was greatly exercised, but, as we were right in the midst of a great "break" in the meetings, I could not bring myself to decide to go home.

While giving my little sweetheart anew to the Lord, the suggestion came to me: "Telegraph father." My father knows how to "pray through." I at once telegraphed the facts to him at Wilmot. He received my message the day before the date set for the operation. On that day I received this telegram from my father: "I have heard from heaven. The doctors will not operate on Ruth." I anxiously awaited a letter from home, and it came two days after, saying that the doctors came ready to perform the operation but found Ruth so much better that they decided to postpone it, and that Ruth was sitting up in bed on the day the letter was written.

The cheerful little lassie is with us now (1917), and the operation remains "postponed," there being no evident need for it.

B. F.

"Not One Chance in a Thousand" for Recovery from Typhoid.

In May, 1914, my wife returned home from a surgical operation in a local sanitarium. Nine days afterward she developed fever. The physician said at the beginning that her health being already in a weakened condition, it would be very difficult for her to recover. The third or fourth day the physician said he thought it was typhoid, and asked for another physician to be called for consultation. The two agreed on the diagnosis of typhoid. The physician suggested an additional nurse and warned me that there was not one chance in a thousand for recovery.

I went to the Great Physician, and laid before Him the five children and His own cause, which I believed was at stake. It was my first all-night in prayer, I pleaded the Lord's promises. About daylight I received assurance of definite intervention, and a short while afterward I went into the sick room in confident hope and faith. The nurse met me with an astonished expression, and said that a most wonderful thing had happened,—"The fever is gone, and your wife is resting quietly for the first time." A slight temperature came that afternoon, but it did not shake our faith. There was no more temperature after that, however, and in three days she was sitting up, and she is still well and strong.

There is not the slightest shadow of a doubt as to Divine intervention in this case.   M. E. D.

Peaceful Submission to Surgeon's Knife.

In the summer of 1913 Mrs. E. was taken to the hospital to undergo a serious operation. Before leaving the home, and again at the hospital the afternoon preceding the operation, we prayed together and definitely committed her to the care and keeping of our heavenly Father.

At a little before three o'clock the next morning she awoke and could not return to sleep. A great fear took possession of her heart as she thought of her coming operation. What if the thread of life were snapped while she was on the operating table, and seven children left behind without a mother? Ought she to take the risk? The fear became agony. Then she reached for her Bible lying on the little table by her bed and opened it with a prayer for some special promise. The Spirit of God immediately directed her eyes to Psalm 56:3. Reminding the Lord that her trust was in Him, she asked Him to rebuke the spirit of fear and fill her heart with His peace. The deliverance came quickly, and in a few minutes she was asleep again. At nine o'clock she was wheeled into the operating room, the surgeon felt of her pulse and said, "Well, surely here is the pulse of a Christian, for you are just as calm as if you were being wheeled out to breakfast."

The sequel to this experience of Mrs. E. was the fact that two saints living in different parts of the city and unacquainted with each other, yet both friends of Mrs. E., were awakened that morning at three o'clock, and both upon awakening felt at once the impression that they ought to pray for Mrs. E. This was remarkable, as neither of these friends were in the habit of awakening at that early hour. It is needless to add that they both at once remembered her before the throne, and had the satisfaction of knowing later that their prayer had been marvelously answered. The operation was successful, and Mrs. E. was spared to her husband and her children.   R. L. E.

A Child Delivered from Chronic Bronchitis, Following Whooping Cough—the Worst Case of the Kind.

Our little boy a year and a half old was very sick with chronic bronchitis, following a severe case of whooping cough. Afterwards, the physician, who was of unusual ability and very successful with children, told us that this was the worst case of the kind he had ever had in a very extensive practice, and that he doubted being able to bring the little fellow through. The mother and I both had special experience in nursing, and were giving every care possible. The doctor was coming two and three times a day.

I said one day to the mother, "What shall we do? The doctor and we are doing everything possible. Must we take him to another climate?" Like a flash came the "still, small voice." "You are trusting too much to your experience in nursing and the good care being given and the fine doctor you have. Bring him to Me." We had been praying about it often, and had thought we were looking to God for the help needed.

An errand called the mother from home for a little while, and stronger still and sweet came the tender drawing: "Just bring him to Me." I took the little fellow up in my arms and literally "brought him to God" in prayer, not so definitely for healing itself, as that I the father was just taking him and the whole case directly to God and resting it all there. It was this, and not a question of doctors and medicine vs. faith healing; just bringing the little sufferer in his extreme sickness to God and leaving all with Him. Sweet peace and rest came at once into my heart.

I put the baby down, remembering that the doctor had said, "If his fever is still up at two o'clock, give him another dose of oil." I did so, for his fever was up and had been for days and days, while the child steadily grew worse. The case was now God's, and I went about the Sabbath's work. That was the last medicine he had or needed. His fever was gone almost immediately, he was resting, and in a few days he was well and hearty after weeks of severe sickness.   J. W. A.

A Sick Child Recovers.

This incident is a leaf from the experience of a pastor in one of the hard fields of a great city. The mother of the child in question was a Christian, having been converted a short time before the illness of the child which threatened its life. Indeed, its ailment was pneumonia and this was made the more dangerous because it followed a long, stubborn case of whooping cough. Several of the older children were in the Sunday-school, but the father was an unbeliever. He was a good-natured, care-free, indulgent parent, inclined to laugh off everything of a serious nature. He was a salesman, and his business drew him in daily contact with the rough element of the stables and livery barns throughout the city. He was a moderate drinker, though in the eight or ten years of our acquaintance I never knew him to drink to excess. All the effect religion ever seemed to have was to amuse him. He attended church regularly with his wife because of his Scotch training, but he was perfectly indifferent to all the appeals of the Gospel.

However, when the child became dangerously ill and was given up by the doctor, nurse, relatives and neighbors, and a gloom had settled down on the home, while the child was hovering between life and death, I paid the family a visit. I found the father in tears and the mother almost heartbroken. Naturally, I was sympathetic, but was at a loss to know what to do. I was glad to see the father in a serious frame of mind and took the occasion to speak to him closely about his relation to Christ. I do not know why, but while I was talking to him I was prompted to say: "If I pray for this child and God allows this crisis to pass and recovers the child from its illness, would you take that as an indication of God's goodness to you, and also an evidence that He wants you to turn from your sin and live a Christian life? I am not certain that the Lord has caused this shadow of death to fall upon your home in order to bring you to repentance; but He sometimes uses such means when other measures fail. Now what do you have to say to my proposition?"

After a little while he replied, "What you say might be true and if the child should get well I would consider it an act of providential favor and I think I would be willing to be a Christian."

With this understanding I began to pray and I had not proceeded far in my prayer before there came upon me such a powerful unction, that I felt instantly my prayers were being heard, and before rising from my knees I had the assurance that faith had prevailed and the child would recover.

The child did recover and as far as I know is still alive and well, but it was full four days before any kind of a change was noticed. Those were days of testing, but faith never faltered; that my prayer had been heard and in due time would be answered, I had not the slightest doubt. While all others expected nothing but death, and talked of the impossibility of the child's recovery, I had the courage not only to expect but to talk of its full restoration to health, although I had to do this against appearances and the judgment of the doctor who was an old practitioner and a skillful physician.

Sure enough, at the end of the fourth day, a change for the better was noticed and the child was snatched from the gates of death where it had been hovering for several days. The father was deeply impressed by the evident answer to my prayer, but did not immediately surrender his life to Christ. He has since joined the church and, as far as I know, is living a consistent Christian life.

C. P. M.

"Call unto me, and I will answer thee, and shew thee great and mighty things, which thou knowest not" (Jeremiah 33:3).

God's promises are given not to restrain, but to incite to prayer. They are the signed check, made payable to order, which we must indorse and present for payment. Though the Bible be crowded with golden promises from board to board, yet they will be inoperative until we turn them into prayer.—*Meyer*.

CHAPTER II.

PRAYER FOR FINANCIAL AID.

Missionary's Prayer for Money Reaches Across the Ocean.

There was a great need of money for certain things in regard to the gospel work in Africa. Prayer had been made for some time, but the money did not come. It seemed it must come, but no help arrived. One morning at devotions the missionary could not leave off praying, and worship lasted about twice as long as usual. When he opened the mail that day there was a letter from a bedridden saint in Pennsylvania, in which she said, "I have felt the pull of your prayers, I hope this meets your need." There was a check for just the amount he had been asking the Lord for. He had been praying in Africa and a saint in Pennsylvania, America, felt the "pull." What a faith!

C. H. C.

Railroad Fare Provided at Time of Need.

I was invited to conduct a series of meetings. When the day for my departure arrived I found myself without enough money to pay the fare. Between my room and the station there were twenty men from whom I could, upon the merest suggestion, secure all that I needed. But I was learning to trust God, and my prayer was that if He wanted me to go to D— He would have the money for me at the station. With confidence I packed my bag, and walked to the train. Stepping up to the ticket office, I asked what the fare was to D—. "Two dollars," was the answer, and as the words were spoken, a man reached over my shoulder and laid two silver dollars down upon the counter in front of me.

G. C. G.

Financial Aid Through a Bible School.

I went from a business life to the Bible Institute of Chicago to prepare for the ministry, arriving with ten dollars. Soon I was reduced to four dollars. I very earnestly asked God for help, and he led Dr. Torrey to do an unusual thing—give an untried young man a scholarship. Then I needed money for my mother whom I had taken care of for several years, and the editorship of "The Institute Tie" was turned over to me, and I was thus enabled to secure the money needed.

Again I needed money and I told God that I was obliged to have some by a certain date, and on that day I was given a cap full of silver and bills—the collection taken for services rendered in an evangelistic meeting. It has been my experience through over twenty years of increasing need in the care and education of my family that God has increased my salary as my needs grew larger. Never has He failed to supply all my needs "according to his riches in glory by Christ Jesus."

E. L. B.

Money Received for Home Necessities.

I was engaged in special meetings in New York when a letter from home told of pressing financial need there. This need was taken at once to God. The arrangement under which I was working was such that all moneys put into my hands were turned over to the institution with which I was connected and which paid my salary. I reminded the Lord of this and asked that, in sending me the money for which I asked, it be made especially clear that it was for me.

Five days later I went out of the city to speak at an evening service, and was a guest in the home of a friend at that place. After dinner, as we were preparing to leave for the meeting, my host put a beautiful pocket Bible into my hand, inscribed as a gift, and said, "The check inside is payable to your wife. I intended it for you, and knew that you would not keep it if payable to your order."

I then told him of my prayer, and he said, "I was strangely impressed to make the check in that way. You will observe that it was an after-thought, as the 'Mrs.' is written diagonally, there being no room for it on the line."

G. C. A.

Lifted Out of Debt.

It is almost four years since the Lord Jesus Christ came into my heart, and, oh, how happy I have been since that time! I will never forget the condition I was in before I came to Jesus. I had a good wife and the Lord had blessed us with four good healthy children. I had just got down into the depths of sin. I was head-over-heels in debt. I owed one man $1,500 and another $200, and many other debts. I also had a good business, but was spending more than the business could earn for me. I finally got so bad I really did not know what to do nor how to get out. But, thanks be to God, He showed me a way.

On the 16th of August, 1913, the Lord Jesus sent a voice from heaven, saying, "Do you know where you are going?" And my answer to Him was, "Yes, I am going to hell." A question came again, "Do you want to be saved from hell?" "Yes, yes." I got down on my knees, asked the Lord to forgive me all my sins, told Him all about my debts (which bothered me more than all other things), and, do you know, the Lord has paid all my debts in full and more than that, He has given us a fine home. Thanks be to the Lord Jesus Christ who never leaves us nor forsakes us!

M. T. P.

Church Obtains Money for New Building Without "Raising" It.

This is written in Holy Week, 1917. It pleased the Lord to so bless the work of the Park Memorial Baptist Church (Springfield, Mass.), as to cause a pronounced need for larger accommodations. The church owned plenty of vacant land for a large addition, but none of the needed money for the building was in sight. In January, 1915, a few men were talking about the needs of the church and the impossibility of securing sufficient funds to erect the desired addition. One man questioned, "Did any one of you ever put your feet on that vacant land and ask God for a new building for our enlarging work?" None of them ever had done this. These men then pledged each other that every time they passed the vacant property they would walk out on this portion of land and pray the Lord to give us a building to be used for His glory.

At this writing we have $50,879 in a local bank credited to the Park Memorial Church Building Committee, and there has not been a single effort in personal solicitation. "Call unto me, and I will answer thee, and show thee great and mighty things, which thou knowest not" (Jer. 33:3).

B. F.

God Sends Exact Sum Asked for.

Some years ago, while a student at the Moody Bible Institute, I had a small sum of money which I was anxious to contribute to some one of the many causes there presented.

A most devoted Christian man was at that time giving a course of lectures to the students on prayer. I had heard several of his lectures, had met him once, but aside from his official position knew nothing about him.

In waiting on God for guidance in the disposition of my money, I seemed to get no definite leading, but as I prayed this gentleman came into my mind. Several times this occurred. Finally, I thought perhaps this is the answer to my prayer. But why should I give money to a stranger, who did not seem in need? However, I acted upon this leading, and my mind was at rest. I wrote a note to the man, telling him I did not know why I was to send it to him, and I expected that he would be greatly surprised, but I believed God wanted him to have it.

On the following morning his reply came, in which he said: "I was not at all surprised to receive the money, for on a certain morning and hour I knelt and prayed for exactly that amount." It was the very time that I had first prayed for guidance.

This man of God may read this and remember the incident.

V. C. S.

Money for Missions.

I received a letter from a Jewish mission that my husband and I were very much interested in and to which we had for several years been giving $25. But on this particular year we had given our subscription for Jewish work to another needy mission. The home call for local work and other needy places had been numerous and it seemed we had given to the limit. As I read the letter my desire was to give, but I reasoned "Where is it to come from," and I prayed to the Lord to help me get the money. I pledged $6 and laid it upon the Lord to help me get it, trusting and believing He would.

A few days after we received a letter from a young woman, a Roman Catholic, who had been converted under my husband's ministry. She said she was going to be married and wished to have the minister who led her to Christ perform the ceremony. Right away I thought this is the way the Lord is going to supply my need. Our railroad fare came to $5. I knew they were poor and my husband had not received more than $5.00 for a wedding in twelve years, but on this occasion he received $10. The bride told me that her husband had been praying for two years that the Lord would give her to him to be his wife.

The next day we received another call to a wedding, both parties were consecrated Christians, and my husband received a fee of $10. The bride told me that she knew her wedding was in answer to prayer. As my husband had made it a habit to give me all his wedding fees, I now had $15. I asked the dear Lord for $6 and He gave me $15.

F. C. L.

Prayer Brings Church a Needed Thousand Dollars.

While I was pastor of the Arlington Presbyterian Church in Baltimore, Md., we were praying for a new building, which was erected before I left there (costing $60,000). Before we could secure certain funds for the new building it was necessary to pay off the balance upon our land, amounting to about $1,000. I had drained the organization to the last penny, and felt that I could not ask any more of my people. One Sabbath morning I spoke upon the fact that "prayer changes things," and so burdened did I become with the sense of the need of prayer that I turned the whole morning service into a prayer-meeting, and a number of men and women led in prayer, asking specifically that God would provide the $1,000 needed. At the close of the service a young woman who worked in a factory as a forewoman, and one whom I thought had little of this world's goods, came to me and said, "Could you meet me downtown tomorrow evening, as I come from work, at 6 o'clock. I want to give a little to God's work."

promised her I would. And the next evening I met her. She said, "Pastor, the devil has been tempting me all day not to do what I'm going to do, but God is laying it on my heart to help in His work, and I want to give you this, but no one is to know who gave it." I thought she would give me five or ten dollars at the most, but to my utter surprise she handed me a $1,000 bill. She then told me her father and mother had died leaving her a few Baltimore ground rents, and she felt she ought to give this to the Lord for His work. Needless to say we paid the balance due on the ground and built our church, without recourse to any secondary methods of money-raising, such as fairs, etc.

G. A. B.

A Pastor's Need Supplied.

It was late Saturday evening. The week had been one of unusual blessing as well as real testing of our faith. God had shown Himself favorable in giving several messages that brought souls into the kingdom that week. But now the week was about gone and we were really "up against it," for our supplies for the kitchen were vanishing, and had nothing in the house for the coming Lord's day. What should we do, or to whom should we go? We waited on God and then committed it to Him, knowing that "He is faithful that promised." About eight o'clock that evening a young woman came to the house, and after a few words of greeting told us of the evangelistic meetings in the nearby church. Then, in a way that seemed to embarrass her very much, she spoke of the Lord's money that she had.

She had intended going to the meeting, the one she mentioned, and before going had prayed about giving this particular sum of money to the evangelist at that place. Then she told us how God whispered to her heart and told her to give it to the pastor (the writer) and his family. "But," she protested, "they would think it very strange for me to come to them with money." So, she said, she told the Lord that she might give one-half of it to the evangelist and the other half to the pastor. But the same "still, small voice" repeated what she had first heard, and the impression was so strong that she knew "it was the Lord" and so came to us with her story. Then in a way full of apology and embarrassment she handed me the bill, asking me to take it as coming from Him.

It was received with thanks, and was "sufficient" to meet "all our need" for the days following, and gave us a new assurance of His faithfulness and that our God will supply all our need by Christ Jesus.

H. W. L.

Protected from the Winter's Blasts.

About twenty years ago the writer lived in North Dakota, serving home missionary churches as missionary and evangelist. As a family we needed a place that we could call home—"be it ever so humble." After securing an acre of ground in the town of Niagara, in the spring of 1897 we started to build a house, but it took nearly a year to finish it. Winter came on (and they are usually severe in that state), with the house unfinished. Snow-storms and cold biting frosts made the chills creep over one. I was away from home at the time this peculiar incident happened.

Our youngest child was a baby in the cradle. My wife and the three children were really uncomfortable, on account of not having storm-windows, which are an actual necessity in that region. Three days of storm, snow, and frost set the missionary's "better half" to thinking. One morning, while standing at the table washing the breakfast dishes, the thought came to her of the heavenly Father's care for the least of His children. She lifted up her heart to Him in prayer, and in simple faith told Him her need—then, just forgot about it, waiting and trusting.

In less than two days she received a letter from a friend, a widow, who is a devoted Christian woman. This saint lived in a town about forty miles away. In the letter there was a check for $25. The note said in substance, "My dear Mrs. McQ.: I have been thinking about you all day, and I am wondering if you are not in need of something which I can supply. Enclosed you will find a check, with love, ——" Of course, wife and children had cause to thank the heavenly Father and rejoice. Within a few days the storm windows were secured, which added much to the comfort and delight of us all.

N. McQ.

A Financial Crisis in School Days.

When I left home to enter college my best asset was a new-found love for God. Peter's fervent avowal, "I dearly love Thee," daily renewed itself in my own life and experience. But the lesson of God's great love for me—His solicitous care for my little life—somehow failed of any particular impression upon my mind until the following incident brought it home to me.

A financial crisis had arisen during my course. My small savings were almost exhausted and the proceeds from my "self-help" efforts were not enough to make up the deficiency. The school year was so far advanced that to drop out at that point meant a bad set-back. I needed at least $100 to finish the year. There seemed no human prospect of my getting it. At last I announced to my two room-mates that I would have to quit. I recall that after the closing lecture of that crucial day I shut myself up in my room and pleaded my cause with God. No relief came. I determined to find a position, and go to work.

Early next morning I took a suburban train to Chicago and began the weary search for employment. A panic was on, and hundreds of young men were bent on the same errand as myself. But at the end of a fatiguing day I found a place, to begin work the next morning. The next day was Saturday. I worked until noon, when the establishment closed for the week. Returning to my student quarters in the afternoon, what was my astonishment to be told that I need not go back to the city on Monday! God had answered my prayer! All unknown to me a Chicago business man whom I scarcely knew, had sent through his brother, a fellow student, the first installment of $125 which he freely placed at my disposal for personal needs. Thus I was enabled to finish my school year, and the way which led ultimately to the ministry was kept open. I have never doubted that this was a direct answer to prayer. I. M. G.

One Hundred Dollars Provided for Miscellaneous Bills.

In Denver, Colo., one New Year's morning, a godly man and wife, living in a modest brick cottage, footed up their bills due by the tenth of the month, and found that they amounted to about one hundred dollars. They had met with misfortune and did not have any money left. But no one knew they were in need. They knelt down and pleaded for $100 before the tenth of the month, that they might not injure God's cause by not paying their debts.

Before the tenth of the month, no one knowing that this man and wife were without funds, there came a letter from a business man in Colorado Springs, stating that, knowing that this man had had some financial reverses, he would be glad to lend him $100, without interest, as long as he needed it; and requesting the friend to write and tell him of his exact financial condition. There went back a letter that afternoon, telling that he had nothing left, and enclosing his note for $100, payable with interest, three months from date.

There came back to the Denver man the next day from

Colorado Springs a letter stating that the business man, on balancing up his books on January first, found he had on hand some cash he did not need for the present and that that morning, while in prayer as to what he should do with this money to the glory of God, he was deeply impressed to make the Denver man a New Year's present of $100, but not knowing that he was in need. He was afraid to write and offer the gift, but knowing that no business man would object to another offering to lend him money, he had first written and offered to lend the money; but that he enclosed a check for $100 as a New Year's present as prompted while in prayer on New Year's morning, at the very hour when the Denver gentleman and his wife were praying for $100. T. T. M.

A Faith Mission and Its Wonderful Support.

As the treasurer for twenty-three years of the Central American Mission I could write a whole book on direct answers to prayer in carrying on its work.

Organized at the home of Dr. C. I. Scofield in Dallas, Texas, November 14, 1890, at a little prayer-meeting with three laymen, its fundamental principle was to solicit neither missionaries nor money from any but the Lord, and this has been strictly adhered to.

The Lord has sent into this field about one hundred missionaries, and has called out from its converts about the same number of native helpers. He has sent through its treasury $220,000 and about $50,000 from the native churches and believers, notwithstanding their deep poverty. Every missionary entering its service agrees to depend solely on the Lord for the supply of every need. We do not have many startling or dramatic answers to prayer, and yet month by month the Lord supplies every need, and during these twenty-six years we have not known of a single missionary who has suffered actual need, and some have been on this field more than twenty years.

The mails in these lands are often uncertain. Some two years ago the drafts sent to Miss Laura Nelson of Dulse

Nombre, Honduras, were taken from the mails, and for more than six months she did not receive a cent from the treasurer, and yet in answer to prayer the Lord increased the products of her garden in flowers and vegetables, and gave her a good market for the same, so that she says the Lord heard our prayers and supplied all our needs from this unusual source.

The outfit and passage money of nearly every missionary that has gone to this field from the beginning has come in direct answer to prayer, after the missionary was ready to go.

At the beginning of half of the months in the life of this mission the treasury has been virtually empty, and yet by faithfully waiting on the Lord in prayer the supply has been sent in by Him before the end of the month.

D. H. SCOTT.

Help in the Day of Grief.

The missionary had been away to preach and was coming home on Monday. Home was the place where a true wife, the mother of a dear baby lived, away up by the big mountains. The missionary expected the wife and baby would be on the porch, if not at the train, to meet him; but no, they were not to be seen. His heart sank as he entered the house and saw a limp little body in the mother's arms. The doctor said it would take some days to determine what was the matter. Anxious, trying days passed and the missionary and the little mother watched, waited and prayed that their little one might be spared, if that was God's will. Then the doctor said one word—"Typhoid." Days dragged into weeks and the little body grew thin, the little smile grew fainter, and the little voice weaker, until there were just two words that came again and again from the parched lips: "Amen" at the close of each prayer for his sweet life was one. "Happy," was the other, and the little mother sang over and over, by day and by night, with a grief-stricken heart, and tear-filled eyes, but with a steady trust and with as steady a voice as she could command,—"There is a happy land, far, far away." Then the doctor said two words, "No hope."

Money was painfully scarce with the missionary and his wife. They wanted, so much, if the baby died, to take his body back east and bury it by the side of another little body. The mother began to pray, "Lord, please send us money, so we can bury the darling beside the other little grave."

Meanwhile three people 1,700 miles away were watching the mail for news. Three days after the doctor said, "No hope," three people in an Eastern state sat down to lunch. One said, "Any news?" The baby's grandmother said, "There is no hope for the baby, and those people will need money." Within twenty minutes of the time that "Jesus called the little child to Him," a boy brought those stricken parents a message that $150 had been raised to help in their need.

And so, just a week from the day the life left its pretty casket of flesh, a little white casket, covered with flowers, was let down into the earth beside a little grave where lay the precious dust of the little brother whom God had called to be with Jesus years before. At the service the loved ones in the East saw the dear face, and two sweet voices sang, "There is a happy land, *not* far away."

D. S. M.

Flour When Flour Was Needed.

My first call to a pastorate was to a needy mountain section in California, where the church membership was small and infidelity abounded. I went to the place with the understanding that they could not pay me a salary, but that I could receive the collections (which amounted to about $15.00 a month) and with this amount I was expected to support my family of five and pay six dollars a month house rent.

Realizing that it would take great faith as well as works, my wife joined me in praying for an increase of faith and Divine guidance, promising to trust God for our daily bread, and that we would not go in debt for food or raiment. All went well for a while, but finally the test of our faith came when one morning my wife informed me that we were out of flour. As I did not have the price of a sack of flour, and recalling our promise to God that we would trust Him, I took it to the Lord in prayer and was assured that my prayer would be answered that day.

At noon we ate what was left of the morning meal, and about supper time a Christian woman who resided in San Diego, forty miles distant, came to the door with a sack of flour. She informed us that early that morning she was impressed with a feeling that she must drive to her brother's, who lived a mile beyond our home. In order to reach her destination she had to pass near by the old ranch house which she had vacated a few months before, and which had not been occupied since; so she turned aside from the main road to visit the vacant home, and while passing through the rooms she found a sack of flour in one of them, which she put in her buggy and started on a distance of eight miles to the home of her brother, where she would tarry for a visit.

While she was pursuing her journey with the sack of flour in the buggy, she said that, as she was praying and praising God for His goodness and mercy, the Spirit impressed her to take the sack of flour to Hobson's. So strongly was she impressed to do this that she asked the Lord to guide her horse to the place where He wanted the flour to be left.

When she finally came to the by-road that led to the parsonage, her horse, unguided by visible hands, left the main traveled road and came and stopped in front of the parsonage door, with the sack of flour. When she learned that God had made her a special messenger to supply a special need, she came in and broke bread with us and tarried until the morning. This incident created a profound impression upon the infidels and other Christless folk, and many were convinced that there is a God in heaven who hears and answers prayer, for they knew all the parties connected with this incident.

T. H.

Provision for Unpaid Taxes.

In the stress of work I had wholly forgotten, even to the day after Christmas, that my taxes, amounting to about $96, must be paid on January 1. I had just reached Ashville, N. C., for a brief rest. The matter of the unpaid taxes came to me as a great shock as I was resting in bed the morning after Christmas. I immediately called my wife for a consultation. I suggested an absolute trust in God to give the funds according to Philippians 4:19. It would have to come from Him, as I had nothing, and there was nothing due me from anyone. I also suggested a loan of $100 from a friend in the North who had assured me of his willingness to help me in any time of need. The money could be borrowed and things honest provided, but it would have to be paid back and I had no stated income on which to depend. We agreed to trust it to God to do and the matter was sealed by united prayer. About ten minutes after the prayer, the postman left several letters and the first one among them was a letter from that very friend in the North and in it was a check for $100, with the brief statement that he wanted that share in my work.

"And it shall come to pass, that before they call, I will answer; and while they are yet speaking, I will hear."

L. S. C.

A College President Proves God.

Some years ago a college president sat in his office, striving to outline the duties of the day. The door opened, and the librarian and head of the English Department entered, with a story of much need in the way of books for the library with special adaptation to the work of the English Department. It was argued that the president had provided a full equipment in lines of science but had been rather meager in library advancement. Inquiry brought out the fact that about $750 worth of books would greatly relieve the situation. The college treasury was empty, and salary demands more than equal to all prospects of income, yet here was a palpable need. After a moment of silent prayer, the president said to the librarian, "Order the books you have mentioned. I do not know how the money will come, but this is a real need and the Lord will supply it." The librarian departed with a satisfied smile.

Turning to his secretary, the president dictated to a prosperous business man the following letter:

"Dear Friend:
"Some seven or eight years ago I wrote you a letter concerning a matter of beneficence, to which you made so gracious a reply that I somehow feel I am not making a mistake in writing this letter. A good man said that the way to raise money is to ask God and tell His people. I have asked God concerning this, and am now going to tell one of His people. Our library needs are pressing, and for efficient work in the English Department about $750 worth of new books are essential. I have thought that you might be interested. If for any reason this plea should seem to you unreasonable, please set it down to college insanity, and do not let it interfere with our friendship."

The letter was written, and, before sealing, the president and his secretary bowed a moment in prayer, asking God to use the letter as an instrument for His work. Some days passed and there was no answer. At times there came almost a fear that the request had been wrongly made, and then followed a quiet reliance on God and the prayer that he would lift the burden of anxiety, and not allow this to sap the energies that should be devoted to college efficiency. At the end of a week the response came. The president read the letter without glancing at the check enclosed. It said:

"Dear Friend:
"In response to yours of November 17th, I am sending you the enclosed check to be used any way you may desire. Kindly incorporate with your own personal account, and transfer to the treasurer in such a way that my name will not appear in the transaction."

The president then turned to the check with the eager hope that it might be $800, so as to allow the purchase of a library index, or even $1,000, so as to enlarge the book purchase, but behold it was for $10,000, proving that its sending was under the direction of Him "that is able to do exceeding abundantly above all that we ask or think." Other claims were pressing, and these were joyously met. Ordinarily it is wrong to purchase anything until the money is in hand, but in this case God's direction was clear, and the answer according to "the multitude of His tender mercies."

R. McW. R.

God's Providence in Supplying the Temporal Needs of Missionaries and Candidates.

Twenty-two years ago a gracious answer to prayer came to us in the China Inland Mission Home in Toronto and my wife often wondered who had been used as God's messenger for the supply of our need. Only this morning (August 6, 1917) the long-standing question was answered in an unexpected letter from an old friend now living in London, England.

We had often noticed that whenever missionary candidates were in the home God allowed a time of shortage which cast us wholly upon Him and made very real to the new workers what the life of dependence upon God meant. Such seasons were not our normal condition; but when the testings came they were made times of much blessing.

My friend's letter mentions the fact that Mrs. Merry of the Annie Macpherson Homes had visited the Marylebone Presbyterian Church with a company of the children, to entertain a number of aged women under the care of the church. Mr. Mowle, who is missionary in connection with this church, spoke of the time when he and his wife stayed in the China Inland Mission Home in Toronto, where their eldest son—now wearing the military medal for bravery in France—was born. Mrs. Merry was interested to find that he knew us and she was led to speak of Nellie D., who, at that time, was our faithful nurse maid, and of her brother George, now a business man in Toronto.

It transpired that George D. has always traced his success in life to an act of faith which he performed at a time of crisis in his career. He was out of employment and was searching diligently but in vain for work. Nellie was out with our two children on the Saturday and she met her brother who told her that he had found no success. He had called at one business house, however, where they had said that he might come in and inquire again on Monday. Nellie tried to cheer her brother by telling him that at the Mission Home they were also being severely tested even in the matter of food, but that God had always been faithful in answering trustful prayer. This thought dwelt in his mind as he returned to his boarding-place. Whilst he prayed to God to open up his way by giving him work to do, he thought of what his sister had told him.

As a young helper in the mission family, Nellie had not yet come, as she did very fully in later days, to understand the principle of not making our needs known to man, and in this case God used the utterance which we could not have sanctioned.

George paid his week's board bill and then found that he had some fourteen dollars left. He put a five-dollar bill in an envelope and came round to the Mission Home. There he found some children playing in the garden. He gave the envelope to our three-year-old daughter Winifred and told her to take it to her mother. When she did so the mother asked her who gave it to her, and all she could say was, "Man gave it to me." Mrs. S. had just been on her knees asking God to send money to buy milk for the children, at least, and here was God's loving answer to more than her petition. The whole household was filled with praise and fresh acknowledgment of God's loving care. Nor did George's act of faith go unrewarded; by his gift he had made his own dependence upon God more definite.

When Monday morning came he went back to the firm whom he had visited on Saturday. They still had no settled position to offer him, but they needed some one to run the elevator for a short interval, and he was willing to fill any post temporarily. This resulted in his obtaining a settled engagement with this firm later on. He is still with them and occupying a very responsible position. F. A. S.

The promises of God are certain, but they do not all mature in ninety days.—*A. J. Gordon.*

God Supplies Financial Needs.

In the early days of a pastorate in a mission field in one of the slum districts of Chicago, I became sorely in need of money. My salary was very small and irregularly paid. I had just married and was trying to set up housekeeping and furnish a home. I came to a place where I needed $10 to meet a certain obligation coming due. My month's allowance was not due for several days and I needed money at once,—that very day, in fact. While casting about for some avenue of help I remembered the liberal offer of a gentleman connected with the congregation supporting the church of which I was pastor, extending to me the privilege of calling upon him whenever I was in need. This was about the last thing I would ever think of doing, but in my emergency I was sorely tempted to apply to him for help.

Before calling on the gentleman, however, I made the matter a special subject of prayer, and not knowing what better to do I called at his office with the intention of asking him for the amount needed. I think I must have sat in his office for more than an hour. Several times I attempted to speak of my need, but was unable to do so. On my way home I upbraided myself for being a dunce and letting such a splendid opportunity for getting the help I needed go by without availing myself of it. While in this mood it occurred to me that I should call and see a man for whom I had performed a certain service and whom I had reason to believe was interested in the subject of religion. It was just a pastoral call I had in mind, but when I was leaving he took out his pocketbook and taking a five-dollar bill from it offered it to me, saying: "I owe you something for the services you rendered me recently." I protested that he owed me nothing and tried to refuse the money, but he insisted that I should take it as he was quite able to give it and even more willing than able. Being thus urged, I took the money.

On leaving his home I congratulated myself that half the amount needed was in hand, and wondered how I was to get the other five dollars. From his home to where I was living was about five blocks and I was just about to walk into my front door when a friend encountered me and said: "I have something for you which I have been carrying in my pocket several days, hoping I might meet you." While he was saying this, he produced a five-dollar bill and handed it to me saying: "This is for that little service you rendered my sister some weeks ago. She told me to hand it to you the first time I saw you." Again I protested that I did not wish any pay, for it was my custom not to make a charge for the kind of service I had rendered. However, he was urgent and pressed it upon me. I finally took it for I could see plainly that this was God's way of providing the $10 I so much needed.

The coincidence was so remarkable that I was sure God was answering my prayer. I could have gone home another way and missed this man and at the same time would never have thought of visiting the other. As it was, had the second man been a moment later I should have been in the house and out of sight.

How true it is that all God's trains are on schedule time! He never fails to make connection with His trusting children.

C. P. M.

"No time to pray!"
Oh, who so fraught with earthly care,
As not to give to humble prayer
Some part of day?

"No time to pray!"
'Mid each day's dangers, what retreat
More needful than the mercy seat?
Who need not pray?

"No time to pray!"
Must care or business' urgent call
So press us as to take it all,
Each passing day?

What thought more drear,
Than that our God His face should hide,
And say, through all life's swelling tide,
"No time to hear!"

—Selected.

CHAPTER III.

PRAYER FOR DELIVERANCE IN TIME OF DANGER.

Prayer Answered in Time of Approaching Fire.

I was living in Maysville, Ohio, many years ago and we were in reduced circumstances owing to the illness of my late husband. Our little all was invested in our store and our furniture, none of which was insured. A great fire broke out across the road from us, and we were in great danger. Our neighbors tried to save our place by wetting carpets and putting them on the roof. My little daughter came to me, and said: "Mother, pray." I looked up and said, "O God, turn the blaze, and save us." Instantly God answered, and the wind which had been blowing from north to south turned in a moment to blow from east to west. Our house and store was spared and almost all the street was rescued by this answer to believing prayer.

Mrs. J. W.

A School Boy's Experience.

That was a lonely day when I had been at school in Lee County (Ala.) "Rocky Ridge" Schoolhouse in 1869. I was asked that day to memorize seven pages of ancient history and informed by the school-teacher that missing one word I would have the "hide taken off my back." This all happened when eleven years old, and while the teacher, with his eyes dancing in his head like yellow lights, pointed me to my seat and fixed the next morning at ten as the hour of recitation.

Over that lonely mountain road, with tears in my eyes, I wandered, and reaching home soon informed my precious mother of the impossible task and the doom awaiting me next day.

For once I found that no human help could avail. Mother sat up late trying to coax into my head the triumphs of Cæsar and Hannibal. The fear of coming punishment deterred me from memorizing one answer on that seven-page history lesson. Mother persuaded me to retire, rise early when memory would be fresh and the lesson easy. I retired, but sleep fled; my flesh was cold and clammy, yet rising I fell to the study, but alas of no avail. My hope sank. I could even then feel the seasoned hickory cutting great long red furrows in my quivering flesh. Mother said, as she handed me my little tin dinner bucket: "There is one chance for you, my son. Go down into the woods just this side of "Rocky Ridge" Schoolhouse and ask God to help you learn the lesson, for He is a God that will answer your prayer."

Over the lonely road I trudged with steps of lead, reaching the deep pine woods within five hundred yards of the school. I took mother's advice and crept down under a great pine tree, crying to God as a poor boy all undone and helpless, for assistance to learn the long lesson. In a moment, like a flash, I was conscious the help had come to me from the eternal world, my first message that ever went through to God and my first conscious answer from God. I sprang up with new life and bright hope, my mind working like lightning. I ran to school, opened the history and literally ate the seven pages of history, kernel and core, until the teacher called me at ten o'clock. My answers were so perfect that the irate teacher looked me over (a rapture betrays itself) and said: "Young fellow, you saved your hide; go to your seat."

It was God that answered my cry that day. The discovery and the answer were far ahead of Marconi for he was not born. The distance must have been from beyond the sun; over 95 million miles, even from the third heaven, and Marconi has not talked over 6,000 miles as yet. My message went over space without battery, wire or poles, not even a relay, not one cent of expense, and no outlay except a breaking heart, and a faith deathless and resistless.

H. W. H.

Deliverance in Time of Danger 45

Railroad Engineer Saved in Wreck.

Along the line of the Southern Railway, between Greenville, S. C. and Atlanta, Ga., there goes a limited train driven by one of the best engineers on the system, whose name is D. J. Fant. "Dave," as he is familiarly known, is not only an engine man who knows his business, but he is known far and wide as a most earnest Christian, and a splendid preacher of the gospel of Christ. Humble and consistent, prayerful and earnest, he has the confidence of all the men of the road from the president down. It is my privilege to count this man among my closest friends in gospel bonds.

Two miles from the town of Toccoa, Ga., through which town this railroad runs, there is a high curved fill on the side of the mountain. Up in the hills some distance was a little summer hotel where I occasionally spent portions of the summer with my family. Fant was at that time running a fast mail train which on its southbound trip would pass this fill near ten o'clock at night, and he said to me, "Miller, when I get on the big fill I will blow you a signal each night I go down, and when you hear it you may know I am praying for you." So many a night ere retiring I have gone out on the upper piazza of the hotel to listen for that signal, and then send up a prayer for the man at the throttle who was also remembering me at the same time.

Some time later Fant's run was changed to a limited Pullman train passing this place in the afternoon. One day when he struck the curve at regular speed he felt instinctively that there would be a wreck, as the track workers had been engaged in repairs and had left the track in such condition that he knew the engine would not stay on the rails. He called to his fireman to jump for his life, and he did so, rolling down the steep embankment and coming out with many bruises but fortunately no broken bones. Dave stayed at his post, and sure enough the ponderous engine soon left the rail. As he was rounding the curve ordinarily it would have turned over to the right which would have crushed him, but after running over the ties a short distance it turned to the left, and instead of rolling down the embankment, it plowed its way down, several cars plunging down behind it. Fant stepped up through the open window, and found himself standing amid blinding smoke and hissing steam, on top of the overturned cab, without a scratch of any kind. None of the sleepers was overturned, and not a passenger was hurt. The conductor from the rear car looked out when he felt the jar, and saw the engine plunging down across the curve of the fill. He afterward testified that it looked as if some great cables of some kind were holding her to keep her from rolling.

Being at Spartanburg, S. C., at the time, and seeing an account of the wreck in a paper, I telegraphed Brother Fant at his Atlanta home, using in the message Psalm 91:11, 12: "He shall give his angels charge over thee," etc. The same day Fant mailed me a clipping from an Atlanta daily describing the wreck, and on the margin he had written, "Psalm 91:11 and 12." In answer to prayer God had sent His angels of deliverance.

How remarkable, and how like our God that at the precise point where so many nights His faithful servant on this railroad engine had sent his prayers up to the throne while at the same time sending his signal out over the hills to another fellow servant, this mighty deliverance had come to him in a time of impending death!

Fant still lives at 400 Capitol Avenue, Atlanta, still runs his engine, still prays and labors for his Lord, and wherever I go in my services I tell this story of his faith and God's answer, and many others are cheered and encouraged to continue to call on God. R. V. M.

Lost in a Canadian Bush; Delivered.

Yesterday (August 24, 1917) I had a very trying experience and a marked answer to prayer. We are spending a few weeks on the shores of Lake Huron, at Ipperwash Beach, where we rent a cottage. I started out early in the morning for a walk and to find the best place to pick wild blackberries and raspberries. I left the lakeside and followed an Indian trail, expecting to come out at a village. Instead of that, I got deeper and deeper into the forest, and when instead of reaching the lake shore I came to a swamp which I could not cross, the conviction that I was "bushed" came upon me.

After struggling for a long time I came to a little open spot where I sat down and watched the declination of the sun, in order to get my bearings, and then started in the right direction. I found it impossible, however, to keep straight, for there was no real walking but only desperately toilsome struggling and crawling between and under trees and bushes. After a long time I came out into a little clear spot, only to find that I had gotten back to the place where I had sat down. Now I lay down almost exhausted and told the Lord that I was baffled. I asked him to show me a way in the wilderness, and I took comfort from His promises. "Fear thou not; for I am with thee: be not dismayed; for I am thy God: I will strengthen thee; yea, I will help thee; yea, I will uphold thee with the right hand of my righteousness" (Isa. 41:10) seemed wonderfully appropriate just then. I shouted again and again in hope that some Indian might hear me, but there was no response.

The clouds gathered and hid the sun, and the rain fell heavily for an hour or more. I was wet through and my shoes were full of water from sinking in the swamp. As I struggled on and on without knowing which way I went, I rather wondered why the Lord did not deliver me quickly, for I was in a very miserable plight and saw no way of escape. Then I assured my heart again of God's faithfulness and prayed for patience even if deliverance were long delayed, and for strength to go on struggling. I committed myself to God, asking Him to guide the steps that I was quite unable to guide. In this time of entire despair—so far as my resources went—and absolute dependence upon God, I prayed particularly for early rescue because of my wife and children's anxiety, and the trouble that would be caused if the neighbors had to be aroused to search for me.

Forced back by an impassable swamp into the almost impassable jungle, from which I thought I was escaping, I stood for a time in utter dismay, and then praying and trusting I started again with the determination that I would struggle on as long as the Lord maintained my strength. From this point deliverance began. I had only struggled in the thicket for a few minutes longer before the ground began to rise and I came to a place that had at some time been cleared. Now it was overgrown with a dense tangle of brambles and raspberry canes. It was with torn skin and clothing that I fought my way through, but in half an hour or so the tangle thinned out and to my joy I saw the faint old tracks of a cart. These I followed carefully for only a short distance and then I emerged onto a road and the lake lay just beyond. My heart was full of thankfulness to God as I turned for the three-mile walk back to our cottage. The strenuous exercise prevented any harm from my wet clothing, and when I reached home I found that some of the family had just started out to search for me.

F. A. S.

Coal Miners Delivered from Explosion—A Remarkable Deliverance.

In December, 1911, I conducted a revival in Coal Creek, Tenn. Coal Creek is the railroad center from which spurs run out to the mines in the mountains. Saturday morning I was called from the breakfast table to the telephone. The Methodist preacher was on the other end of the wire. In a very much agitated voice he said: "Brother Hicks, there has been an explosion in Cross Mountain Mine. I have a number of members in that mine and think I had better go up there. Would you be willing to go with me?" I replied in the affirmative. In a moment he was at the door with a horse and buggy. I climbed in and we drove up the valley to old Cross Mountain.

I can never forget that drive. It was a beautiful December day in the Southland. The leaves were stained red in the blood of the dying year. The squirrels were hopping along the roadside gathering their supply of winter nuts. The birds seemed to sing with pathos, as if they were touched with a feeling of our sorrow. We rode silently until we came to a sign saying, "Miners, buy your whiskey at—." My friend said, "Brother Hicks, that is solemn mockery in an hour like this." Evidently some one else thought the same for the sign was broken down as I passed back.

Soon we met some miners in caps and overalls and sooty faces, evidently just out of a mine, running down the road. We asked them, "What about the explosion?" "We're from Thistle Mine," they replied, "There is an entry from our mine to Cross Mountain. Some of our boys were blown down on their faces but no one hurt." "But what about Cross Mountain?" we asked. "Oh, blowed all to pieces," they replied, and ran on down the road.

A little farther we came to the string of houses that make the mountain village. What a bedlam of sounds we heard! Women were crying and praying, children screaming and old men shouting excitedly. One woman with a baby in her arms ran out to our buggy and cried, "Oh, for God's sake, do something to reach my husband and get him out of there. I don't see how we can live without him." "We'll do anything in our power to save him," we answered as we drove on.

Soon we rounded a spur in the mountains and got the first view of Cross Mountain Mine. It was a drift mine, entering quite a distance up the side of the mountain. Dust and leaves were floating slowly out of the mouth of the mine. The idle power house stood near by with the smoke curling lazily from its stack. Everything looked grim and silent as if the old mine were sulking after its deed of cruelty.

A Thrilling Scene.

Such a scene I never expect to see again this side the judgment! At one end a woman sat on the ties of the tramway screaming, "O God, if he'd only been ready to go!" Another stood near her twisting the ropes, her face as pale as death, not uttering a word. An old man wearing a mackintosh walked up and down the tramway crying, "My God, my poor boy." The people became so frenzied that it was necessary to make a door and put it over the mouth of the mine lest some irresponsible person should slip in. One poor fellow rushed up to the door crying, "Let me in, let me in. I want to go to my brother!" They led him away stark mad.

After the men had been in the mine two days we gave up all hope that any of them should come out alive. By and by they began to bring out the dead. Mr. Wood, a leader in our campaign, went to his sister, Mrs. Henderson, whose husband and boy were in the mine, and asked her: "Where do you want Bill and the boy buried when they are brought out? I think they will reach their entry today."

"There'll be time enough to talk about burying Bill and the boy when they are dead," she replied. He said, "Oh, you might as well give up. They're all dead; they couldn't possibly live in there this long." She looked at him for a moment and answered, "Bill and my boy are not dead; I haven't been on my knees two days and a half for nothing." He thought she was going crazy. He asked some neighbor women to watch her.

Upon his own initiative he had the graves dug where he thought she would like to have them buried. That night after supper Mrs. Henderson went into the kitchen and put some water on to heat. The watchers asked her what she was going to do. She said, "I'm heating some water for Bill and the boy to wash with when they come out." They said to her: "Mrs. Henderson, they've had an explosion, and they're all killed; none of them will come out alive." "Oh," she replied, "Bill and my boy will be out before ten o'clock tonight."

Between nine and ten o'clock that night, somewhere in the bowels of old Cross Mountain, a rescue party had their lights go out. They were asking one another for a light, when a poor fellow behind some boards and mud plaster that had been put over an old entry to keep back the bad air shouted to them: "I'll give you a light, if you'll break down these boards." Quickly they tore down the boards and there stood Bill Henderson! He had come down from a room a little farther back where he, his boy and three others had barricaded themselves, and spent the hours fighting back the choke-damp and praying. Most of them, not expecting to get out alive, had written farewell letters to their loved ones. These five came out before ten o'clock that night. Of the eighty-six souls that went into Cross Mountain Mine on the morning of the explosion they were the only ones who came out alive. I. E. H.

Deliverance from a Sinking Steamer in Mid-Atlantic.

Doubtless the most remarkable answer to prayer coming into my experience was the rescue of the S. S. "Spree," with Evangelist D. L. Moody and party aboard. It occurred in mid-Atlantic, December, 1892.

When nearly one thousand miles from land the driving shaft of the steamer broke, causing a break in the after part of the hull into which water poured, and for three hours it seemed as though the vessel must sink.

The officers and engineers succeeded in closing the bulkheads of the three forward compartments after three hours' hard work. The captain announced he thought they would remain afloat until help came, unless they had severe weather. He had steered a southern course to avoid the winter's ice and now was drifting farther out of the regular track of the steamers. They drifted helplessly for two days and nights out of reach of any passing means of rescue. During the day signals of distress flew from the mast-head and all night flare-lights burned and rockets were sent up; but Sunday morning dawned with no help in view.

By the captain's invitation every one was to assemble in the saloon for a prayer meeting, to be led by Mr. Moody. He read the 91st Psalm and verses 23-31 of Psalm 107. Mr. Moody had often said there was a promise of God to cover every phase of human experience. They never had to pass through that experience before, but when they did the promise to cover was there to be claimed. They claimed deliverance, prayed and what was the result?

One hundred and fifty miles away (this was before the days of wireless telegraphy) the S. S. "Lake Huron" was steaming eastward. A splendid Christian and native of County Dublin, Ireland, was her captain, and I was a passenger enroute to join Rev. Merton Smith in continuing work started by Moody and Sankey. The prayer meeting on the "Spree" had hardly ended when Captain Carey came to ask me to hold a meeting that night. All entered heartily into the service and we sang, "Pull for the Shore," "Throw Out the Life Line," "Let the Lower Lights Be Burning," and other hymns of the sea.

Our service ended about 9:30 and I was taking my walk on deck before retiring, when the boatswain's mate accosted me. The meeting had evidently impressed him for he said, "I am going round to see that our lights are trimmed and burning brightly, for it may be some one will be glad to see these lights before morning." Surely words of prophecy!

The second officer, on the bridge shortly after midnight, was attracted by the illumination caused by the flare-lights on the "Spree." Thinking it a ship on fire he called the captain who came to the conclusion, after observation, that it was a ship in distress. "Change our course, Potter, and let us bear down upon her and see if we can render assistance, for we may be in need of help some day ourselves." We came alongside after steaming two and a half hours.

About three o'clock Monday morning, after two vain attempts, made in the darkness, to throw a line aboard, we signalled, "I'll stand by until morning."

At dawn God seemed to speak to the waters as He did once before, "Peace, be still." And the wind ceased, and there was a great calm." A boat lowered from the "Spree" brought an officer on board to tell of their desperate condition. Captain Carey offered to take them in tow, and should that be impossible, he would endeavor to transfer the passengers and crew to his vessel. Refusing to bargain, he promised, with God's help, to do all in his power to save all on board the disabled vessel.

Because of the calm the bringing of the tow-lines from the "Spree" and making them fast to the "Lake Huron" was accomplished without further mishap and a start made for Queenstown.

Would the lines hold should a storm break, and would our coal supply last, were problems pondered by the captain with these seven hundred lives now dependent upon him. With a strong faith he brought us daily nearer land, and five days passed without mishap. Friday noon, while in conversation with him, I learned he expected to see the first light on the west coast of Ireland at eleven that night. Seeing neither sun, moon, nor stars, for days, yet perfect were his calculations.

Steaming into Queenstown harbor at five o'clock we signalled, "Drop anchor." Captain, officers and crew of the "Spree" gathered on the forecastle deck of their steamer to cheer the captain and crew of the "Lake Huron;" and I never again expect to hear the like. It is remarkable, to say the least, that the "Lake Huron" did not have sufficient coal to keep her steaming another fifteen minutes and was forced to coal up before proceeding to Liverpool.

I made my way immediately to the cable office to notify friends of my arrival. Here I met Mr. Moody, who exclaimed, "Hello! Bell, where did you come from?" "I was on the 'Lake Huron,' I replied. "You were!" cried Mr. Moody. "I was on the 'Spree.'" Calling to the crowd he said, "Here is a friend of mine, who was on the 'Lake Huron,' he'll tell us all about it"; and pushing me up on a chair, he insisted upon my telling how God had answered their prayers.

As I got down, he said to me, "Bell, was your captain a Christian man?" I said, "Oh, yes, a splendid Irish Methodist." He replied, "I thought so. I knew God would have one of His own to send to our rescue."

J. R. B.

"In my distress I called upon the Lord, and cried unto my God: he heard my voice out of his temple, and my cry came before him, even into his ears" (Psalm 18:6).

He that is much in prayer shall grow rich in grace. He shall strive and increase most who is busiest in this, which is our very traffic with heaven, and fetches the most precious commodities thence. He who sends out oftenest the ships of desire, who makes the most voyages to that land of spices and pearls, shall be sure to improve his stock most, and have most of heaven upon earth.—*Archbishop Leighton.*

CHAPTER IV.
PRAYER FOR GUIDANCE.

Led Into and Equipped for Christian Service.

When I was a young man about twenty-three years of age I believed the Lord had been dealing with me and seeking to lead me into Christian service. But as I had no special theological training I did not think that I was fit for the ministry, and I tried to excuse myself for the same reason that Moses did under similar circumstances. I was a man of slow speech and of slow tongue, but the Lord answered this objection in the same way that He answered Moses, "Who hath made man's mouth? have not I, the Lord?" I then made it a matter of prayer, and I believe in answer to prayer the Lord led me to enroll as a student in the day courses of the Moody Bible Institute of Chicago. Truly the Lord's ways are not our ways. I have great reason to thank God for leading me to such an institution.

J. D.

Led to Make a Journey of 2,000 Miles.

On one occasion, believing I was led of the Holy Spirit to make a journey of over two thousand miles to engage in gospel meetings, and being without the necessary means for my transportation, I received the assurance while at prayer that I must get ready for the journey.

With my suitcase packed I started for the train and before I reached the station a stranger presented me with a round trip ticket from Los Angeles, Cal., to Chicago, Ill., good for eight months. While on this journey I preached in several cities, and led many to accept Christ. One of the cities I visited was

Miami, Okla., and while engaged in a brief campaign there I was led of the Spirit to go to Lowell, Kans., and that very day a man from Lowell came with his horse and carriage after me, saying the Lord had sent him to take me to Lowell, to hold a revival in the academy.

E. L. H.

Guided to Brethren in Need.

During a revival in the city of F., one night at the close of the service, while I was praying, I was strongly led to go at once to the city of A., which was several miles away. I hurried to the station just in time to catch the interurban car going to the place. While I journeyed on in the night I prayed for guidance, and was comforted and encouraged with the belief that God was leading and the journey would not be in vain.

Upon reaching the city of A., I left the car at the station near the center of the city, and before I reached the sidewalk a man called out, "Here is Mr. Hobson," and there before me were three men who told me they were in need of some special spiritual advice which they believed I could give them, but not knowing where I was they had met in an upper room and asked God to send me to them that night and were so sure their prayer would be answered that they came to meet this car believing that I would arrive on it.

E. L. H.

Call to the Ministry Confirmed by Opportunity for Preparation.

At the age of eighteen I felt God's call to the Christian ministry. I explained this to my parents, but my father, being a commercial man, discouraged it. He said he needed me in his business. I sought a message of guidance from the Master and found it in Psalm 37:5: "Commit thy way unto the Lord; trust also in him; and he shall bring it to pass." I did the committing, and daily prayed that He would "bring it to pass." I said no more to my father about the matter, but four years later he voluntarily said to me: "If you really desire to give your life to Christian service, you may." Then he added, "And if you wish to go to the Moody Bible Institute in Chicago, you may." This was a double answer in prayer. I do not remember that I ever told my father of my desire to attend the Institute, and as we lived in England, I felt that such an honor and blessing would probably never be mine. But God brought it to pass, and, overwhelmed with gratitude for this remarkable answer to prayer, I became assured that God not only hears our petitions, but can do "exceeding abundantly above all that we ask or think."

P. W. S.

James 1:5 Appropriated for Education.

My father went to heaven before I was fifteen; I was the oldest of four children and mother was in broken health. Father's life insurance had lapsed and our farm was mortgaged for its full value. I went to work in a store for $50 a year and board; and my brother soon went to work for another storekeeper at similar wages. Mother had taught us to seek a good education—but how?

In the first Bible that I bought with my own earnings I read in James 1:5: "If any of you lack wisdom, let him ask of God." I asked for an education. I had never seen a college. Later I rode a thousand miles and climbed College Hill with $30 in my pocket and the promise of a loan of $75. Four years later I graduated, and my brother along with me. He went on to one university and I to another, and we both got through. He is a Doctor of Medicine; I am a Doctor of Divinity.

At our family altar I taught our children to pray for a good education every morning. God has answered, opening their way and supplying their need. Three of them are through college and are teaching others; the forth is in the senior class; the fifth a freshman; the two youngest are nearly through high school.

God answers prayers that are right. Let the poor and the fatherless and everyone hope in Him and strive always to please Him.

E. A. B.

An Unruly School Subdued.

It was a country school, but one of the hardest in the county, and the writer's first year as a teacher. The man who had taught the school two years previously was regarded as one of the best in the county, having had several years successful experience, but this school had proved too much for him. The large boys had banded themselves together and had put him out bodily and locked the school-room door on him. And a repetition of this disaster was threatening the writer, for things were rapidly going from bad to worse.

Nothing effectually availed; and finally, as nervous system and everything else seemed going to pieces, recourse was had to a night largely of prayer. Oh, what a night—it will never be forgotten! Morning dawned, but the burden was still there, heavier than ever. But just as the sun was rising, the writer being still on his knees, suddenly the entire burden lifted, and prayer was answered and every step of the way to school that morning (a mile or more) was one of praise. The boys and girls were all there, but it was as if their natures had absolutely changed. The room that day was perfectly quiet, perfectly orderly; and even more, it marked a turning point. For from that day forward there was scarcely any more trouble whatever. "Call unto me, and I will answer thee."

S.

God Hears the Prayer of the Boy in Trouble.

My first recollection of God hearing my prayer goes back to the time when as a bare-footed lad I lived with my parents on a farm. A few days before I had been presented with my first jack-knife, in those times quite an era in a boy's life. That morning, while playing in the pasture, I had lost the precious knife and had spent over two hours in a fruitless search for the same. When my mother called me in to dinner my heart was too full of sorrow over my loss to care for any. It flashed into my mind that the Lord knew where that knife was, then why not ask Him to show me where it was? The only prayer that I knew up to that time was my evening prayer that I always repeated on my knees by my bed before retiring. That was the only place for prayer that I knew, so while the family were at dinner, I slipped into my bedroom and kneeling by my bed I poured out to the Lord my trouble and asked Him to lead me to where the lost knife lay. I got up from my knees, dried my tears, and with full confidence that I would find that knife, ran out again into the pasture, and walked straight to where I picked up the knife, about twenty-five yards into the field.

I was too young to understand the theology of prayer, but I well remember that that day I had an overwhelming sense of the fact that God was interested in a boy's troubles, and my heart was filled with gladness.

R. L. E.

Concerning a Change of Field.

Upon several occasions I have had blessed answers to prayers concerning change of location. An account of the latest may be helpful to my brethren in the ministry.

Several years ago I accepted a call to a certain city to do missionary work, with the promise that after a year or two I should be given the class of the English Bible in the college which was located in that city. I labored for more than three years, but the Bible teaching did not open up for me. Meanwhile, city mission work had been pursued with mingled success and seeming failure.

At length the day came when this door also suddenly closed. Nearly everything seemed to go against us and our hard work to come to naught. We were being sorely tried. My wife and I consulted together and then knelt side by side and laid our case before the Lord, confessing any mistakes we might have made, urging our past loyalty to Him, and acknowledging our complete dependence upon Him. Even while we knelt there came the full assurance that our prayer was answered.

Six weeks or more passed for the further trial of our faith. Then came a letter from the president of a college situated near both of our old homes, offering me the very work for which the good Lord had all along been preparing me, a work which I am still happy in performing.

G. S.

Guided by a Sign.

While superintendent of a large Sunday-school I left a very successful business career to equip myself for a large field of usefulness in the Sunday-school field. In devious ways I was led out of the office of superintendent, and had several alluring calls to other forms of Christian service. Prayer failed to open these doors. I was determined not to preach.

One day a friend 'phoned me to call and see him. The object of his invitation was veiled. It turned out to be an offer of any one of three pastorates then open.

My "thorn in the flesh" for some years had been a troublesome throat with hoarseness. It came to me that this affliction might be the answer to my problem of whether I should preach or continue in Sunday-school work, which offered me several positions.

Accepting the pastorate of a very small church, I asked God for a sign as to my future labors for Him. If my throat continued to trouble me, I should take it as a sign that I was to continue in Sunday-school work. If my throat affliction disappeared shortly, it would be a sign of approval upon my preaching, and I would continue. Taking up the ministry in November when my throat was always most troublesome, the hoarseness and soreness disappeared at once, and during the almost five years of that pastorate never returned. Content to minister to a small congregation, I am assured of God's seal upon my chosen life-work.

E. L. R.

Prayer Answered for Employment.

Just after the World's Fair of 1893, at Chicago, in the extremely hard times of the winter following, I was out of employment and earnestly seeking work as a young man almost unknown in the country's second largest city, when many thousands more were out of work and desperately seeking it. The halls and corridors of the City Hall and other public buildings were opened to shelter men who could not find a place elsewhere those bitter cold nights to sleep.

One afternoon in January I went up into the Y. M. C. A. parlor, knelt down alone, and prayed very definitely for God's help and guidance in finding work. I started at once to see a man who was wanting agents—a kind of work to which I was not adapted and in which I could hardly have "made it go." Down on Madison Street, walking west to see him and thinking that that might be the best I could do, something seemed to stop me on the sidewalk and say: "Better go and see the other man first,"—a man whose advertisement I had seen in the paper. As I hesitated a moment, having my mind pretty well settled for a try at the agency work as about the only thing for me, the voice in my heart seemed even more clear and almost audible: "Better go and see the other man first." I did, turning and going directly east to his office. He gave me a good position and I worked there over five years in a place of great responsibility and opportunity, having my salary increased several times and gaining a most valuable experience for a young man in business.

God's plan was by far the best, His guidance direct, and His answer immediate.

X. Y. Z.

Power of Prayer in Sorrow.

I remember that from early childhood the great mystery of life to me was sorrow. How could the nearest and dearest be taken away and it be possible for the human heart to endure? As the years passed this mystery grew only the more mysterious. As I saw the quiet strength of some of God's children at such times, and as I came to know some of the marvels of His grace and loving kindness, I often questioned, What can He do for one? How is it possible? And then there came a day with a message from one so well-beloved, one the loss of whom had never entered the mind, the one who could not be spared—and she must die! She could live but a few days.

Doubtless, there are few who read these lines but know the agony, the pain of it, the thing that could not be, that must not be, where could there be any refuge from such a storm? I do not remember anything that I prayed, just reaching out to the One whose love had been so often proved, and it was as though I could feel the "everlasting arms underneath" and could hear His whisper, "I am going to do some beautiful thing for her"—and His quiet and peace stole into my soul there to abide. There has been often the sharp pain of the loss, but never again the impossible "must not be."

Of the many, even daily, proofs I have had that "prayer changes things," this stands out as the most precious. As I see so many sorrow-stricken ones who seem not to know this place of refuge I long to "be able to comfort them . . . by the comfort wherewith I myself am comforted of God."

Mrs. F. H. H.

Directed to a Field of Labor.

There are a few things that the writer learned while in the Moody school at Chicago which left a deep impression. One of them was a lesson on the secret of guidance given by Dr. F. B. Meyer, and may possibly be found in his book of like title.

He illustrated it in this way. He said that when the boats were going into New York harbor there were three lights that must be kept in line in order to enter with safety. If one light was out of line, they were in danger. So, he said, in the matter of guidance, there must be a strong inward impression that we ought to do a certain thing, or go to a certain place—but since all inward impressions were not of God, we should not believe every spirit but try the spirit whether it be of God (1 John 4:1-3). Second, the voice must be in harmony with the Word. His Spirit never leads contrary to His Word. Satan may sometimes quote isolated passages, as to Jesus (Matt. 4:6; Ps. 91:11, 12).

Third, the opening up of Providence. He opens the way. We do not need to break down barriers or burst open doors (John 10:4). When the impression is from the evil one these voices will never agree.

When I was ready to leave school three fields were open, or were asking for my consideration. After praying over the matter I felt quite confident as to which field the Lord would have me go, but the other fields continued to write, and one of them wrote me to be there to preach on the coming Sunday. The more I thought and prayed about it, the more I felt sure that this was not the field. So I talked with my wife about it, and we together took the matter to God in prayer. Before the evening meal a telegram came, saying not to come, that they would explain later, while $42 came from the first field (where we felt sure God was leading) to pay our way. Hence, the opening up of Providence. I did not know for some years afterwards why the telegram came from the field saying, "Do not come." Thank God, all things work together for good to those who are the called according to His purpose.

G. E. D.

God Uses a Dream for Blessing.

While pastor of a church in the West I dreamt one Saturday night that the head of one of our families, a man I had recently taken into the church, was in dire distress. The dream made such an impression upon me that I repeated it to my wife in the morning, remarking that I felt like calling him up on the telephone. I refrained from doing so, however, but noticed that he was not at church that day. The next afternoon, while coming with my wife out of a public building, we came face to face with the two daughters of this man, and suddenly remembering my dream I said to the younger, "How is your father?" A startled look came to her face, but after a moment's hesitation she replied, "O, he's quite well, thank you." "Which goes to show," I added, "that dreams go by contraries, for I had a bad dream about your father night before last." We went on home.

Fifteen or twenty minutes later there was a ring at the front door. It was this young woman, this time alone. She was deeply agitated and immediately sank into the chair I offered. At once unburdening herself, she confessed that all was not well, as she had lightly pretended, that my question had pierced her conscience, that she must come and tell me the truth. She and her father, to this time always comrades, had had a terrible quarrel and had not spoken to each other for several weeks. The father, already burdened by other matters, was driven almost insane by this unhappiness, and, as I learned later, had contemplated suicide. The young woman went from my house to her father's home, followed her filial promptings and was happily reconciled with her father. When she called me on the telephone next morning, I knew it before she told me, from the note of joy and gratitude in her voice.

Who can doubt that God himself brought that unhappy man up in my dream that night to avert a probable worse tragedy, and to heal the trouble which had separated members of the same family? God moves in mysterious ways his wonders to perform.

I. M. G.

Guidance in Matter of Christian Work.

Many years ago an opportunity came to the writer to go into a lucrative business. All arrangements had been satisfactorily made. I was happy in the thought that soon I would be sole proprietor. I had the savings of a life time entrusted with a real estate and loan agent, and when I went to him for a settlement he informed me that he had put everything in his wife's name, and I was minus the money to make the payment to the man from whom I had purchased the business. I laid the matter before him, and to my great relief he said, as he smiled, "It is all right, my young brother, God knows best, and all things work together for good to them that love the Lord." After prayer for the guiding hand of the Lord upon our future, I left him with a light heart and more faith in my blessed Saviour. The very next morning, after praying for guidance for the day and for an opening either in business or Christian service, just as He saw best, I went out and met the president of the Young Men's Christian Association, and he said, "You are the young brother I have been looking for. I have watched your work at the Mission, where a number have been converted, and the board of directors of the local Association have authorized me to tender you the position." I thanked him and said that I would pray over the matter and if I believed it to be the will of the Lord, I would accept. A few days after waiting upon the Lord I was led to accept that important place, in which I remained nearly four years, where from one to a half-dozen young men were led to take a definite stand for the Lord Jesus Christ every Sunday afternoon. After leaving this Association for a larger field which also came in answer to prayer, the results were even greater. Years afterward I graduated from the Association into the ministry, and this came about in a very unexpected and unusual way, and was the answer to definite praying on the part of a devoted Christian and myself. Now it is a continuous joy to see people turning to the Lord.

F. C. L.

Prayer Answered for Guidance.

For several years the writer (an optician) had in his show-window a printed card, about 11 by 21 inches, bearing a Scripture message. One day an esteemed business friend engaged him in earnest conversation, trying to persuade him that such a card was incongruous in a business house, and would repel people. He suggested the name of half a dozen Christian business men whom he asked me to consult as to the advisability of my scheme. At an early date I interviewed one of them. His reply was, that he had no advice; that it was a matter to be decided by the individual for himself. Leaving him, the next person visited was the cashier of a national bank. In answer to our inquiry, he said: "You have asked my advice. I will tell you frankly that I don't care much for the plan. You do not need to put up a card to let people know about your Christianity. Your way of dealing shows that. My judgment is that you will be misconstrued and that such a card will do more harm than good."

As I returned to my store with a heavy heart I concluded that it would be best to displace the card, but decided that before doing so I would consult the Lord. Although in the past it was not oftener than very occasionally that any comment regarding the card was heard, yet within an hour from my interview in the bank, and while I was engaged with a patron, an assistant came to me saying that a gentleman wished to see me about the Scripture card in the window. Going towards the front of the store, I was met by a man who proved to be a wide-awake drummer from a New York firm with a French name, and in a line of business foreign to our own. He said earnestly, "You are a busy man and I am a busy man, but I just want to shake hands with the man that has the nerve to put that card up in the window." He added a few words as to the possibilities of good in such a card. I said: "Well, that is wonderful," relating the fact of my several conversations. He replied: "Don't let anybody tell you to take that down."

I was awed by the character and timeliness of the message, and the card has remained in its place to this day.

D. T. R.

Prayer and Providence in Leading to Right Field.

In my early Christian life I felt an impression that I ought to go to Persia as a foreign missionary. I went through college with this distinct impression still abiding. The Foreign Mission Board of our denomination had no work in Persia, but the year I graduated the Board had definitely decided to open work in Persia, so I made application and was duly appointed.

For some reason, however, the Board reversed itself and decided not to send missionaries to Persia. I was asked to select another field where the Board was already at work and go to that. I had never felt any distinct impression to go anywhere but to Persia, but my wife had a sister in Mexico, so the families, the Board and we decided that it would do just as well to go there. On the way to Mexico we were in three railroad wrecks, one of which was quite serious, killing a number of people and injuring a large number of others; one of whom was my wife, who incurred slight injuries.

After we reached Mexico everything seemed to go wrong. In addition to that, the church from which I had resigned kept writing that they thought we ought not to have left, and would not call a pastor until we returned. I replied in each case, "we have put our hands to the plow and should not look back."

After about two months and a half my wife and I agreed that if without any intimation on our part the Lord should lead our former church to give us a unanimous call we would take that as His will for us to return. After a little more than a week of this prayer I received a letter from the pulpit committee saying that they had been utterly unable to agree upon any other man for pastor, though several had been "sampled," and they thought I ought to let them present my name to the church, feeling that a unanimous call would be extended. My wife thought this was an answer to our prayer, but it did not seem so to me. I, therefore, declined to answer this letter at all, as we had asked the Lord for a definite, unanimous call in case He wished us to return.

This promise of a call was not the call itself. But without any answer to this letter on the Sunday following we received a telegram saying that the church extended us a unanimous call to return. We started back to the States on Monday, in the full assurance that this was God's will and have never had the shadow of a doubt about it for a single hour since.

M. E. D.

How Conflicting Prayers Resulted.

Having been trained for active business, at twenty-one I was placed in charge of a force of men, and soon thereafter was made secretary of a close corporation, and began to save money. Though gratified with my success, I felt the need of culture; so when I discovered I had a tenor voice, I left for Dresden to study for grand opera. Determined to succeed, I studied hard. I also wrestled with Jehovah in prayer; like Jacob I sought to make a bargain with Him by pledging Him one-fourth of all my income as a star, to be devoted to charity. But, "Thy will be done" and "for Jesus' sake" were phrases unknown to me.

After three years residence abroad, my health broke down, and I returned a sadder and a wiser man. Starting again at the bottom, I was not long in gaining a competency, so I founded a home. Another three years passed. I was almost prostrated by a dreadful tribulation which God permitted to come upon me. My home was broken up. However, I was given grace to rejoice, as by this trial the Holy Spirit brought about my salvation. I was enabled to say: "All things work together for good to them that love God."

I began at once to serve God, especially as a Sunday-school worker. I led a delegation of thirteen from our school to the state convention one year. We arrived the morning of the first day, and at two o'clock that afternoon, Mr. Marion Lawrance, International General Secretary, was scheduled to lead a conference. As he had not arrived, I was requested to take his place on three hours notice. Our delegates held a prayer-meeting, and God did "exceedingly abundantly" that day. After it was over, the "still small voice" whispered: "Have you not been praying for years to be a success on the stage?" I was startled, for I remembered that the convention was held in the Opera House instead of in the new unfinished M. E. Church. Yes, my prayers were answered, but better than I thought.

It had been my custom to review the lesson each Sunday from the platform. Many came early to visit the school before church. On a certain Sunday "Hannah and Samuel" was the lesson theme. On the way home from church, my mother told me that she had consecrated me to the Gospel ministry from birth, and that she had been praying all the time I was abroad that I should not succeed and be compelled to come home. He had answered her prayer, too.

I am the pastor of a growing influential church, in the midst of the coal, gas and oil region of a Western state. I own my own home and rejoice in an invaluable helpmeet. Our son has also been dedicated to the ministry. L. C. S.

Prayer When Money Is Lost.

The writer is in the retail coal business in Milton, Pa., having been thus engaged for the past eleven years. Until a little more than two years ago I had not reckoned God as a partner in my business. Thank God, He is now the Senior Member of the firm. I entered Dickinson College in the fall of 1901 and graduated from that institution in 1905, without having the blessed assurance that Jesus saves a poor sinner like me.

On Sunday, February 14, 1915, during the Nicholson-Hemminger Evangelistic Campaign, I decided to give my heart to Christ. God blessed me wonderfully, and I decided then and there that I would lay all upon the altar and serve my Lord and Master the remainder of my life. God made a general "clean up" on my soul, and I have been growing in grace ever since.

On Saturday, November 11, 1916, I was in my office doing business until about 9:15 p. m. It came time to go home and I had gotten my Bible and other religious literature, books, etc., together in readiness to carry home for over Sunday. Ever since I have been in business I have made it a rule to take my money home on Saturday evenings. I ride a bicycle when the weather permits. On the handle bars and front fork I have suspended a wire basket just large enough to hold a four-pocket leather portfolio which I use every day in carrying my reading matter from the office to my home. After having counted my money and checked up my cash, I placed the money in the leather portfolio. The amount of money was something like $510. I walked to the wheel with lights burning and doors wide open, and placed the portfolio in the wire basket on the bicycle. I stepped back into the office to pull down the blinds and turn out the lights and in an instant my money was gone. Some one evidently had been watching me all the evening, as we learned the next morning. This some one snatched the portfolio from the basket and hurried away.

I took the matter to God at once. I had made some promises a few days before the theft and I did not want to recall them. The next day, Sunday, I spent a great deal of time with God, and as a result the answer came. God's leading took me to a place on Monday morning where I received the necessary amount, $400, to take care of the promises. On the four following Monday mornings I repaid the loan in items of $100 each. God saw to it that the amount necessary each Monday morning was on hand above the amount needed for my personal wants and business.

The writer hopes that his experience and testimony as to the efficacy of prayer may be the means of leading some poor soul to Christ and that some hungry one may be induced to lay his trials and burdens upon Him.

J. H. J.

A Journey Without Means in Sight.

During a certain pastorate I believed it to be the will of the Lord to take my wife and attend a religious conference which was to convene in a city a hundred miles away. Having no money for our carfare and no conveyance to take us to the station at Escondido, some eighteen miles down the mountain side, we presented our needs to God in prayer and were assured that it was right for us to go and that the means would be provided.

We praised God and proceeded to pack for the journey, and that day I received a letter from persons five hundred miles away containing the amount necessary for our trip. The writer said that while he with others were engaged in prayer, their minds turned to us and the Holy Spirit prompted them to send a certain amount of money to us at once. Then without solicitation, a man who did not own a team said he was led of the Spirit to take us to the station, which was eighteen miles away. We consulted the latest time table and found that the train was due to leave at eleven a. m., so we started early and reached Escondido at ten in the morning, and were going toward the station when the train left, much to our surprise, for we had an hour to our credit as we supposed. On arriving at the depot I learned from the agent that he had received official orders that morning that the train would leave at ten instead of eleven o'clock.

Fully believing that God had led us thus far, I was somewhat confused that we missed the train, for I believed that as He put it in the minds of some of His followers who were five hundred miles away to send us transportation expenses, even so could He have told us to hurry a little, because the train would leave an hour earlier than usual.

Because He did not so impress us, I knew it was the time to stand still and wait for further instructions. Accordingly I silently prayed in the depot and got the assurance that on tomorrow we would be shown why we were permitted to miss the train. The next morning we took the train for Oceanside, where we had to transfer to the main line going to Los Angeles. Upon entering the train at Oceanside a man approached me, and with tears coursing down his cheeks, said, "Praise God for answering our prayer."

He told me that while in the mission field in Mexico, their only child died and that they were taking the body to Whittier, Cal., for burial. They fully expected to leave San Diego that day but were detained in the custom-house. Their grief and loneliness were so great that they prayed God to send some one to comfort them on the train tomorrow, and they were comforted with the assurance that their prayer would be answered. So when we entered the train the Spirit said to them, "These are the persons whom I have sent in answer to your prayer." And to us the Spirit said, "This is why I caused you to miss the train yesterday, that you might comfort these bereaved servants of mine who have suffered this irreparable loss in the mission field."

Thus we were led to trust God at all times and to see that our disappointment was His appointment.

T. H.

Choice Between Home and School Duties.

While at college my course was interrupted twice by what I felt to be my duty to parents and home. The second occasion kept me out of school for a period of six months. I was certain of my call to the ministry and was just as certain that I needed a thorough preparation to answer that call. However, the rival claims of Christ and home set up a conflict in my soul which at times effectually destroyed my peace of mind.

As the opening of a new school year approached, this conflict grew in intensity until I was like a chip on the waves, tossed first this way and then that way. One day it seemed that I should go back to school; the next day I was just as strongly persuaded that my duty was at home. I think I can honestly say that I wanted to know the will of God. I felt that I was at a crisis in my life and much depended on the decision I should make. While thus perplexed, I tried various methods in an endeavor to discover the will of God.

One of the experiments consisted in writing "yes" and "no" on a separate sheet of paper, enclosing each sheet in a separate envelope. I was careful to have the same-sized paper, the same kind of an envelope, and an equal amount of writing on each sheet. I then asked an apothecary to weigh them on the most delicate scales he had and mark with a cross the one weighing the heavier.

The result of this experiment gave me peace of mind for a few days, after which the conflict of doubt was renewed more fiercely than ever. I felt like a man with one foot in the air and try as I might I was unable to get it down upon firm ground. I could get no help from my friends, for some would advise that my duty lay in the direction of God's call; others that I owed my first duty at home.

One night about a week before it was time for school to begin, while returning across lots from a meeting I had attended, I was arrested and brought to a standstill by the thought that I did not need to go a step further without settling this matter finally as God would have it settled. It was a clear moonlight night and about midnight when this thought gripped me, and dropping on my knees I took an attitude of entire submission, telling God that I was as ready to go as to stay, that I had no will in the matter and would be pleased to acquiesce in His will whether it was to return to College, or remain at home.

Having thus withdrawn my will entirely and with a conscious

feeling that I had truly prevailed with God, I arose from my knees. Almost immediately upon regaining my feet a verse of Scripture came to me as though spoken by someone at my side. I had never memorized this verse to my knowledge, neither did I know its location in the Bible. Yet, it was as clear to me as though I had known it all my life. The words were these: "No man having put his hand to the plow and looking back, is fit for the kingdom of God" (Luke 9:62). Instantly peace of mind was restored. I made immediate preparation to leave for school. From that day until I graduated I never had one moment's doubt as to the rightness of my course. What was more, God cleared up the difficulties in my home so that I had no further solicitude in that direction. How true God is to His promise: "And thine ears shall hear a word behind thee saying, This is the way, walk ye in it, when ye turn to the right hand, and when ye turn to the left" (Isa. 30:21).

C. P. M.

Believers are not hired servants, supporting themselves by their own work, but children maintained at their Father's expense.—*Bonar.*

It may be your prayer is like a ship, which when it goes on a very long voyage, does not come home laden so soon; but when it does come home, it has a richer freight. Mere "coasters" will bring you coals, or such like ordinary things; but they that go afar to Tarshish return with gold and ivory. "Coasting" prayers, such as we pray every day, bring us many necessities; but there are great prayers, which, like the old Spanish galleons, cross the main ocean, and are longer out of sight, but come home deep laden with a golden freight.—*Spurgeon.*

CHAPTER V.

PRAYER FOR THE CONVERSION OF INDIVIDUALS.

Two Men, Enemies, Reconciled.

In a Texas town two men quarreled over a difference of $16 and were kept from killing each other by friends. Our pianist was a niece of one of the men. The affair was in the way of the meeting. We resorted to a night of prayer, in which fifty people engaged. The niece finally prayed through, and thanked God for their reconciliation. The next night, while I was preaching, Mr. S. started to the front; Judge W. was sitting in an automobile, but he climbed out and the two men met in front of the pulpit, and their hearts melted in the revival fire that swept over the entire town.

L. E. F.

Saved at the Age of Sixty.

J. C. was converted when he was sixty years old. In early life he attended the Roman Catholic Church, but finally seldom went to church. His wife is an earnest Christian and a faithful member of a Protestant church. Under the direction of the Spirit we were led to hold a meeting at his home one Sunday afternoon, and he was happily saved. A few days later he began to pray for direction from God on the tobacco habit, which he had formed when he was twelve years old. Instantly God answered, and said, "Quit in the morning." This was repeated. It was his rule to smoke and chew and he always began the day in that way. The next morning he burned his pipe and tobacco and now he finds delight in testifying how the Lord delivered him from that filthy habit.

C. G. U.

Converted in a Box Car.

In a night of prayer at De Leon, Texas, Mr. W. asked if we could join him on Matthew 18: 19 to pray that his son, who had been away from home for three years, and from whom he had not heard, might be saved that very hour. Sixteen of us agreed. Five days later he read a letter to 800 people, in which the son told him he was a railway brakeman in Oklahoma, and that, while sitting in a box car at the very hour we prayed, he got to thinking about the possibility of being killed in a wreck. Eternity stared him in the face, and there and then he gave his heart to God.

L. E. F.

For the Care and Sustenance of Drunkards Taking Treatment.

In all our forty years experience we have never failed, when led to His word for guidance, to get an answer. Facing, as we have for nearly twenty years the problem of feeding and caring for a houseful of drunkards (13,000 in all have been welcomed to this Home), we have many, many times found ourselves hard pressed but with the need has always come the supply. First of all, has come the needed grace to handle men whose lives had been so badly warped and cursed. The sum of nearly twenty thousand dollars each year has come in answer to prayer.

G. S. A.

Man Prayed for, for Fifty Years, Surrenders.

While holding a mission in a small Western city a staff-captain of the Salvation Army heard of a man living the life of a recluse, shutting every one off his farm and out of his life. She took her year-old baby with her, and the cooing of the child touched the man's heart so that he promised to attend the meetings. He was an old man and had lived his life in sin, but during these meetings he went to the altar and was saved. As he left the

For the Conversion of Individuals 75

altar another old man stepped forward, and with tears in his eyes told how fifty years before twenty-five young people had made a pledge to pray for this man every day. He was the only living one to see the prayers of fifty years answered.

A. J. F.

A Brother Restored While Passing Through Chicago.

I was a student at The Moody Bible Institute, and was informed that my brother was coming through Chicago, and that he would call on me while in the city. He had been a Christian, but had fallen away. I interested another student and, going to my room, we literally fell on our faces before God and earnestly petitioned that a conviction of sin would come on my brother and that he would be restored to God's favor. God answered our prayer. My brother confessed his sin and was once more made whole. He said that while on the train before reaching the city God dealt very definitely with him and that he knew he must come back to Him, or be forever lost.

W. A.

Prayer, with Fasting, Prevails for a Son.

In a town in Alabama, a pastor in his study one afternoon, preparing his sermons for Sunday, felt deeply impressed to go to a certain store and try to lead a certain young man to Christ. He yielded, closed his study, went to the store, and asked the privilege of a conversation, and led the young man to believe on Christ. The young man went home when the family were at the supper table; but as he stepped into the sitting room he found his father alone, and said, "Father, I accepted Jesus Christ as my Saviour a few minutes ago down at the store." The father burst out sobbing, and said, "My boy, twenty-four hours ago I was so burdened for your salvation that I began fasting and praying, and promised God that I would never again taste food or water until you were saved." No one knew of this covenant with God, the father having told no one.

T. T. M.

Prayer Answered for a Schoolmate.

I know that God answers prayer. My first real experience of this fact came in my thirteenth year, when, with the simple faith of a child, I accepted Christ as my personal Saviour. Almost immediately I became greatly concerned about the salvation of my closest friend and schoolmate, who seemed very little interested in spiritual things. I knew not what to say to her, and doubt whether I should have had the courage to speak if I had known. But, oh, how I prayed! So many years have passed that I remember only the facts. In a short time she professed her faith in Christ and joined our church,—much to my joy.

It never occurred to my childish mind that her Christian parents or home training had anything to do with her conversion. I believed absolutely that it was in answer to my prayers, and this has strengthened my faith and encouraged me ever since.

V. C. S.

Asking "In His Name."

"I prayed for my husband's conversion for about fifteen years," said an active Christian to me, "and it seemed that my prayers would never avail. But one day I read the Master's words: 'If ye ask anything in my name, I will do it.' I saw that I had been asking in my own name, and that I had sought the conversion of my husband for my own personal joy and happiness. I abandoned these ulterior motives, and began to pray earnestly in the name of the Lord Jesus, and for His glory alone. In a very few months my husband was saved, and became an active worker with me in Christ's service."

The reason why our prayers are often unanswered is because our motive and method in prayer are often unscriptural. In Jesus' name we have assurance, for, "For the writing which is written in the king's name, and sealed with the king's ring, may no man reverse" (Esth. 8:8; John 14:14).

P. W. S.

Two Sons, Whereabouts Unknown, Saved on Very Day Their Salvation Was Requested.

In the South a woman arose before a prayer-meeting of about one hundred and fifty women and said, "Ladies, I do not believe that God hears and answers prayer, but I do wish to believe in it. Please pray just now that I may be given this faith." They all knelt in prayer. In a few minutes the lady arose, and said, "How it was done I do not know; but I do believe in it now. Please pray just now that God will save my two wicked sons. They are away from home. I do not know where they are, but God does. Please pray that God will save them just now, this very day, wherever they are." Again the women knelt in prayer. At the prayer-meeting the next morning this lady ran into the church, the tears streaming down her cheeks, waving a telegram in each hand, and exclaimed: "Ladies, here they are, a telegram from each of my boys, and they both say they accepted the Saviour yesterday morning!"

T. T. M.

Prayer for a Politician.

In a series of special meetings a burden to pray for the unsaved by name came upon the Christian people, and as one and another accepted Christ great joy filled every heart.

The desire found expression for the salvation of a certain man who lived in the country. He was a politician and a man who let his disposition run riot, even to attempting bodily injury to his fellow servant. A visit was made in his home, though some feared for the outcome. He was as one under the control of an evil spirit, but gave a kind of promise to come to the meeting. Not seeing him there, inquiry was made and it was learned that he was sick in bed under the care of a physician.

This continued for three days, all the while his name was often heard in petition. A second visit was made in the home and he accepted Christ, "was clothed and in his right mind," and was in the sunrise prayer-meeting next morning, praising God.

C. H. C.

A Sister and Her Family Converted.

In the fall of 1888, at Harlan, Iowa, I found peace with God and became active in His service. Such a burden was laid on my heart for the salvation of a dear sister and her family in Nebraska, that I felt impelled to go out to persuade them to accept Christ. The trip was made, but without apparent success. Soon after that I went to Chicago, and later to Ohio, to study for the ministry; but the burden on my heart for my sister and her family was so heavy that I had to pray much of the time, day and night. The family for which I was concerned moved to Council Bluffs, Iowa. They never attended church and seemed utterly indifferent. For several months I set apart an hour a day for special prayer for this family. In August, 1889, a letter came from my sister telling how wonderfully she had been saved. We agreed on an hour to pray especially for her husband, who was self-righteous and bitter against the church. God saved him, too, in answer to our united prayer within a few months, and later the children confessed Christ, and all became active in the church.

P. C. NELSON.

A Banker's Conversion on Same Day United Prayer Was Offered for Him.

An evangelist visiting a wealthy aged couple said to them that they ought to be very grateful to God for surrounding them in their old age with every comfort. The aged wife began weeping, and said that she was grateful, and that her heart was breaking because her son, a prominent young banker, was not saved; that she had prayed for him since before he was born, but that God had never heard her prayers. The evangelist urged that they three pray for him just then. They knelt and the evangelist asked the mother to pray. She prayed very earnestly and then the husband, followed by the evangelist. As they arose from their knees the aged mother looked up, her face bright, and said that she had the assurance that her prayer was answered. In a short time the dinner bell rang, and just as they were starting for the dining room, the young banker came in and told his mother that a few minutes before he had accepted the Saviour, down in the bank.

T. T. M.

A Wanderer Brought Home.

A young man had made a misstep, and it so troubled him that he ran away from home. No one in the family or town knew his whereabouts. Father and mother began praying, and others were asked to pray. All trace of him was lost, although everything possible had been done to find him. Several days elapsed. It seemed as though all hope had gone and nothing would be heard as to his whereabouts. One day the father spent most of the time in earnest supplication. Great agony and tears were manifest in his praying. His burden was for God to reveal the boy's whereabouts, cause him to write and return home. All this seemed impossible, but the father pleaded Mark 11:24. When Satan would tempt and say that it would be impossible, the father would say: "I believe Mark 11:24." All through the day the burden was heavy, temptations were many, but faith strong. The day on which his prayers were so strong and as nearly as can be recalled, while he was praying, the boy wrote a long, penitent letter and in a few days he returned home.

C. H. C.

Prayer Answered for a Notorious Character.

During the summer of 1916 I was led to pray that God might in some way bring to pass the conversion of some unusual character, believing that it would help to awaken the church and at the same time impress many outside of the church. Presently my attention was directed to the most notorious character in our little city. The way was opened for me to speak to him and to pray with him. I gave him some carefully selected literature and also directed him to the Word of God. At about that time we were led to hold cottage prayer-meetings in private homes on Sunday afternoons, and meetings were held at his home on four successive Sundays. He was present at two of them and finally cried out to God for mercy. This transformed drunkard, gambler and fighter has since helped us to win a number of souls for Christ. Through him our church has reached people who had not been accessible to us, and souls are now coming to Christ at our regular Sunday evening services.

C. G. U.

Salvation of Boy, and His Education.

Some years ago, while conducting meetings in Dallas, Texas, I received a letter from my mother in Ohio stating that a young man of eighteen, in whom I had taken great interest, had become discouraged because of his father's opposition to his purpose to get an education and had run away from home. When the letter reached me the boy had been away for five months and lost to everyone who had ever known him. It was given me to pray for two things—that he should be saved, and that he might be sent to me for help in his education.

About six weeks later the boy came to me in my New England home and with the one request that I would help him in the matter of his education. Arrangements were made which were accepted by his father. I was not satisfied, but went on looking to God for salvation to come to the boy. It was two weeks later when he received Christ without any pressure from me. It was a most evident working of the Spirit. He secured the education he wanted and has since been in active Christian work.

I found out from the boy that he, too, was in Texas at the time I prayed. Little did he realize the forces that were pressing him on over the many hard places for a homeless, penniless boy in making his way from Texas to New England. God knew where he was and He found him. God alone could save and He saved him.

L. S. C.

Prayer of Faith, Offered on Street, Prevails for a Father.

Some nine years ago, while holding meetings in Philadelphia, I had just gotten off the elevated railroad to walk two blocks to my meeting. A young man ran up to me, and entreated me to go at once and speak to his infidel father, informing me that his father had just cursed him for beginning the Christian life the night before. I was late, and on the street I just offered a short prayer, telling the young man his father would be saved.

I went on to the meeting, arriving in time to preach. After my sermon I gave an invitation for the people to come to the altar. Many had responded and the altar was about full. After a couple of prayers I started to pray, and was deeply impressed with the request of the young man, and I said, "Lord, remember the father of that young man who stopped me on the street, deeply interested in his infidel father. God save him, and it may be he is in this meeting tonight. If so, save him before he gets out of the house." I was then struck on the shoulder with a hand, and at the same time a voice shouted. "Mr. B., this is my father, who just this moment came to the altar to be saved. He has not been inside a church for years."

This is the most definite and immediate answer to prayer I have ever seen.

C. B.

For a Husband's Salvation.

In a cottage prayer-meeting in a town in South Dakota I was taking requests for prayer, urging those present to be very definite in their requests. One woman asked prayer for her husband, but added: "I know he won't be saved." I said: "I think we will omit that request." She caught the implied reproof for lack of faith and cried, "Oh, yes, God can and I believe He will save him." She told us she had not been able to get him to the meetings in the tabernacle.

Her husband carried his lunch, and she prepared a splendid supper for him, getting the things he liked. After supper she went to him and put her arms about his neck and said: "John, won't you go with me to the meeting tonight?" He said, "I thought you had something up your sleeve. You need not have troubled though, for I decided this forenoon to go." She asked him what time in the morning he had promised. He said it was about 10 o'clock he thought. It was about the moment her faith took hold.

He went with her. After the meeting he refused to go home until he had a conversation with the evangelist, saying to his wife: "I must be saved tonight." And he was. He went out a saved man, and his wife believes God's words—"according to your faith be it unto you."

A. W. M.

Boy in Reform School Accepts Christ After Strange Providences.

While attending a religious convention at Whittier, Cal., I was asked to preach to the boys of the State Reformatory at one of the churches on Sunday morning, and before I had fully realized the unusualness of the occasion I had accepted the invitation.

That evening I was so burdened with my own unworthiness and inability to do justice to an audience of that particular kind, that I spent much time in praying for a special message for an audience of boys the like of which I had never addressed.

While thus engaged in prayer the Spirit of the Lord came upon me and presented to my spiritual vision a boy whom I saw as clearly as though I were looking at him with my natural eyes.

The Spirit informed me that this boy was Freddie Brown,

one of the boys of the Reform School; that I would see him at the service in the morning, and at the beginning of the service I must ask for Freddie Brown to come to the front, and after giving him a personal message which the Spirit would give me at that time, I was then to proceed with the sermon.

This was indeed a test of faith, for I did not know an inmate of the institution, but I obeyed the Spirit, called for Freddie Brown and a boy came forward to whom I gave the message with which I was impressed. At the close of the services, the officer in charge said, "This is a very remarkable incident, for this morning Freddie asked me to excuse him from going to church, but I was strangely impressed that he must go, and now I see that God was leading me in answer to your prayer."

T. H.

Thirty-Three Answers to Prayer During Special Meetings.

"I have had thirty-three answers to prayer since these meetings began," said an estimable lady of wealth and culture in an afternoon service at Seymour, Iowa, some years ago. "Two of these answers," she continued, "came by telephone and one by telegraph today." There was so much definiteness about this statement that I inquired for more details. Most of these answers were to prayers for the conversion of the unsaved members of her Sunday-school class. One of the answers that came by telephone was to prayers on behalf of an absent friend, another telephoned answer was on behalf of two women, both church members and next-door neighbors, who for years had been in a feud and would not speak to each other. They had been wonderfully reconciled to each other that very day. The answer that came by telegraph was to prayers that this lady had offered secretly that her ungodly husband, proprietor of the large opera house in which Billy Sunday had held his campaign some years before, might give us the use of this house, as our meeting had outgrown the largest church. He was over a hundred miles away, and nobody had said anything to him about it;

but he wired: "Offer them the use of the opera house free of charge as long as they want it." This offer was accepted and for some weeks the meetings continued there.

P. C. NELSON.

Prayer for Conversion of a Father Honored.

Immediately following my conversion, the one great burden of my heart was for the salvation of my father, who was not a Christian; indeed, there was not a Christian in all our immediate family or among any of our near relatives at the time of my acceptance of Christ.

As soon as I had learned the most meagre rudiments of prayer, I began praying earnestly for my father and the other members of our immediate family.

One by one, beginning with my younger sister, they gave themselves to Christ until my father, who was sixty-nine years of age, was the only one remaining in our immediate family who had not yielded to the Lord. The burden upon me for his conversion became more intense than ever and several times a day I went aside especially to pray for him. All this time I was writing letters and giving him in them each week my testimony to the keeping power of the Lord. Some of these he resented, but I continued to send them in spite of his objections.

One night, just before entering an evangelistic meeting of a series I was conducting in the city of Sanford, Maine, I received a telegram from my youngest sister saying, "Praise God, father is converted."

In closing this little narrative of one remarkable answer to my own prayer, I perhaps ought to say that ten months before the conversion of my father I received, while praying for him in Pittsfield, N. H., the definite assurance of the Spirit of God that my prayer for him was answered, and from that time I have had no doubts about the ultimate outcome of my prayer.

W. L. C.

The Conversion of "Sport."

I was doing Y. M. C. A. work in a saloon town which was a big railroad center, and a division point, with shops and offices. The saloons had wide-open gambling. The town was controlled entirely by irreligious influences.

One night I was distributing tracts in front of a saloon. A boisterous crowd, led by "Sport," a gambler, tried to mock me. I read the story of the Prodigal Son to them under the dim gas light. They left me and went into the saloon, but soon came back and invited me in to preach. This they did in mockery. But I accepted the invitation, went in, stood on a chair and preached to that howling, drinking, gambling crowd. Finally, I was enabled to get them to listen. As soon as I was through preaching the leader, "Sport," mounted the chair, ridiculed me, said I ought to be dragged to the river by a rope and thrown in (Missouri River only two blocks away). He put it to a vote of the crowd. It carried with a wild drunken yell. I heard the proposition put and the drunken response to it, but slipped through the crowd and when they looked for me was not to be found.

Next day I went back, found my man, talked to him, plead with him to trust Christ. "No, I can't," said he. "I have lived in a saloon as bartender or gambler ever since I was fourteen years of age. Father is a gambler and mother is a sporting woman." I said, "'Sport,' God has laid you on my heart, and I am going to pray for you." The clearest assurance that ever I had up to that time was concerning this man's salvation.

Weeks passed by. I saw the fellow in this saloon and gambling place repeatedly and talked to him at every opportunity. One night "Sport" sent for me. I went to his room. He locked it after I entered. Then he broke down, and cried like a child, begged my pardon for trying to kill me, asked me to show him the Saviour. We prayed and the man trusted the Saviour, and became mighty in leading his old pals to Jesus.

G. W. S.

For a Daughter's Salvation.

Some time ago, we were assisting in evangelistic meetings in a large river town where liquor was plentifully sold. Those most interested in the meetings were very anxious that in an election to follow shortly after the meetings, the saloons might be closed. The Woman's Christian Temperance Union was naturally much interested, and asked me to conduct a meeting for them. I consented to do so, and when a large number of women assembled I told them that I was convinced that they were depending too much on means and people, and too little on the power of God in prayer. I cited a number of cases where God had wonderfully answered prayer, and talked to them on the subject of faith. I saw they were all deeply moved, and I felt called to do something I had never done before in any meeting. I called for requests from each one and requested no one to ask for anything they did not have faith to believe God could and would do, if their hearts were right and it were in accordance with His will, showing them it is always His will that all should come to Him for salvation. They all had burdens, and one after another humbly and tearfully made their requests. One woman arose, and told about her daughter and what a hard case, humanly speaking, she was. She was married to a Jew, but she said her faith had been so strengthened she believed God was going to answer her prayer. As we were going to our knees a woman came in with two little children and sat down near the door. As she had not been in the meeting during the request, and had not caught the spirit of the meeting, I failed to ask her for a request.

After all had prayed and this mother had fervently prayed and even thanked God for answering her prayer, this woman, who had entered late, came to me and said: "Mrs. M., I want to be a Christian." I, not knowing her name, led her to Christ then and there. There was weeping all over the room, and the mother of this woman was laughing and weeping by turns.

Who was this newly converted woman? I found out it was none other than the daughter for whom Mrs. S. was praying.

A. W. M.

An Athlete Converted.

One night in a Western city there came into the meeting a man who was training pugilists and wrestlers for a coming show. He was a man of iron muscles and will. His magnificent form, splendid development, graceful step, and striking appearance at once made him noticeable in any crowd. His business there was not to get help, but to scoff at religion, which to him was only suitable for weak-minded men and hysterical women. The coming wrestling match for which he was preparing, and which was being widely advertised, was monopolizing the attention and interest of just the men we wanted at the meetings. But what could we do?

It was decided to take it to God in prayer and ask Him to break up that match, turn the attention of the crowd to Jesus Christ, and glorify His name in that city.

The coming of that key-man into our midst that night was taken as an answer to our petitions. While he was there many spent the entire time in prayer while the evangelist preached. The Spirit of the Lord laid the truth upon his heart that very first night. When the invitation was given that strong giant of a man deliberately walked to the front, fell down upon his knees, and began to cry aloud unto God to have mercy upon his soul. After a season of prayer and personal instruction by the evangelist, he arose, tears on his face, with trembling frame and quavering voice, and said: "Friends, I came in here to make fun of your meeting. I had boasted that I would break it up before the match came off. I ask you to forgive me. I have accepted your Saviour as mine. The match will not come off. Pray for my wife."

At the close of that remarkable service, the power of which only God could send, he asked me to call on his wife and lead her to accept Christ. I promised to do so the next day, if he would be there too. He promised, and I went. When I came to the door she did not invite me in. I invited myself in. She did not ask me to be seated, I provided myself a chair. She began to ridicule God, Jesus Christ, the Bible, the Virgin Mary, the church—and continued in a rage of blasphemy, bitterness, and awful language such as I had never heard from man or woman before, until I felt my very hair rise in dread of her terrible doom.

I shall always believe that the Spirit of God prompted me to speak some such words as these: "Mrs. —, I command you to stop this blasphemy. You may talk about me all you wish, but I will not sit here any longer and hear you blaspheme the name of my Saviour and my God! I came in here to help you to know Him. I came to enable you by His grace to be the wife you ought to be to this converted husband of yours, and the mother you ought to be to that darling boy you hold in your arms. I bid you good morning!"

To my outraged soul there had been a great shock. I almost felt that she had doomed her soul forever. Yet after more calm reflection, remembering how God had stopped the wrestling match in answer to prayer, I pleaded with God that He would again show the people His power in saving her. The second night following she sat with her husband, her boy on her lap. When the sermon was over, and the invitation given, she came down the aisle, and asked me if I could ever forgive her. I told her it was my God she had sinned against. She fell upon her knees, and amidst sobs and groans found her way into the kingdom of God! It was God's answer to prayer!

H. W. J.

God Hears a Mother's Prayer for Her Son.

The preaching of the Word of God had been blessed during the winter and a number of souls had accepted Christ as their Saviour. The pastor of the church was sitting in his study in one of the Western states, pondering the goodness and mercy of the Lord, when a rap summoned him to the door. One of the mothers of the church wished to have a conference. She, too, had been thinking of what God had wrought, and a new hope, or the old hope, had been fanned into a flame. Would the pastor and his wife go on a journey in answer to her prayer? She had one son left to her; his home was many miles from a railroad and an expensive stage trip was necessary. She asked her pastor if he would not go and preach two or three sermons, and with his wife sing some of the old gospel songs that had been used to bring a number of persons to the Lord.

He felt that the burden of responsibility was too great, and besides they had two children, ages four and two, who must be taken with them, and he was about to tell her so, when with clasped hands she said: "Do not refuse the last prayer a mother can offer for her son!" These words rang in his ears for the two weeks he asked for in which to consider the matter. Six hundred miles, round trip, by wagon, was a long drive, and he had but one horse.

He and his wife and the mother were praying. One day, as he walked down the street, a cow-boy to whom he had been of help met him and said: "I have a string of ponies on the range, and if you want one of them to go with your horse, you are welcome to use it for the summer." A few days later the harness-maker said: "I have a good harness for which there seems to be no call, and if you can use it this summer you are welcome to do so." But there was no wagon. The mother came again, this time to say: "I have saved one hundred dollars towards the necessary expense." How could the chosen messenger say "no" any longer?

The wagon was purchased, and all necessary camp outfit secured as speedily as possible, for it would take eight or nine weeks to cover the miles of mountain road in an effort to answer "mother's prayer." Every step was taken in prayer, for the messengers felt the burden of responsibility, and that they were handling redemptive, that is, blood money.

It is not necessary to say more about the days of travel and the nights in camp, sometimes eight thousand feet above sea level, than that work was always provided for man and team to furnish the money needed to pay expenses. It is impossible to describe the deep feeling of responsibility that took possession of the two the afternoon on which their destination came into view. Nestled at the foot of a towering mountain that stood as sentry for the ages, clustered the cabins.

On the Lord's day the people came to the services, and the folding organ and hymn books were used to good effect. One man and his wife who had come in from a near-by claim said: "This is our first service in twenty-five years," while others said they had been as long a time as ten years without attending a religious service of any kind. Not two or three services were held, as requested, but a service every evening during the week, and two on the Sabbath.

Jesus Christ was presented with all His claims of Deity, and His call for men, women and children to yield to Him, the Saviour from sin. It seemed as if the one man would not yield. Would the long journey be in vain? The vision of the Good Shepherd seeking His sheep "till he finds it" added new fervor, and kindled new faith. The last sermon was preached. The last invitation had been given. The hearts of the messengers could do nothing more but turn to God with a mute, passionate prayer as the final appeal was given. During the silence that followed he rose to his feet, to be followed by his business partner, to say to God, before his fellow men: "I, too, accept Christ as my Saviour and my Lord."

The weary miles of travel on the part of the messengers had not been in vain. The mother's hope and sacrifice had not been for naught. God had been enabled to "answer mother's prayer."

Years have passed and long ago that mother has gone to be with her Lord, but I can yet feel the hand clasp, and see the gleam of hope in the eye of her son as the next day he came to bid us goodby as we started on the homeward journey, and his voice still rings in my ears as he said: "It is my supreme purpose in life to live for my Lord." And as I raised my eyes above his head it was to see the sentinel of the hills, that had forced its head far above the timber line, standing as a mute witness of that sacred vow to God and man.

C. R. S.

CHAPTER VI.

PRAYER FOR REVIVALS.

Increasing Prayer, Increasing Results.

A friend began a meeting in a country school-house in haying time. The only Christians in the community were two young women. He asked these young women if they would pray fifteen minutes daily for the saving of souls in that community. They covenanted together. Meetings continued, but no power was manifested. He called the girls to him and said, "Girls, we will have to pray more." They increased the time to thirty minutes daily. Still no apparent results in meeting. Finally they agreed to pray forty-five minutes daily for the meeting. Still power was at low ebb. They increased time in prayer to one hour daily.

At this juncture I happened along and was invited to help in the meeting. The power of God fell on the whole community. The interest spread and spread. In that community forty-five heads of families were saved besides hosts of young people, and the work widened out, reaching the surrounding country and the city some miles distant, and still continuing to touch other farming communities in the county. After twenty years had passed it was recognized to be the greatest work of grace in the county, and the beginning was attributed to the prayer of the two young women and the one layman who started the meeting.

G. W. S.

Assurance of a Revival in a Dead Town.

The following incident was told me by a pastor whom I helped in a revival meeting.

He said he had on his charge three preaching places, one of

them called, "Old Salem." At one time the church had been a very spiritual church, but on account of removals, deaths, and at that time spiritual indifference and worldliness, some of the membership were on the point of disbanding the class, as they could with difficulty hold the Sunday-school together and but few attended the preaching services.

One day the pastor visited an older member, who had been sick for some weeks. After a time spent in visiting, then closing the call with a season of worship, the pastor was about to leave, when the man said: "Brother Foster, since I have been sick, and sitting here in my chair, I have been looking up at 'Old Salem' and I have been thinking of the good times we have had there, and of the many souls that I have seen converted. I have been led to pray for 'Old Salem,' and God has given me the assurance that we are going to have a revival at the old church yet. Just you go on, and don't be discouraged, and when you can get around to us hold your meeting, for I am firmly convinced the Lord will send us a revival."

The pastor left the home feeling that in some way light was coming. He did not get around to begin the meeting until late in March. People were very slow about taking hold, but they went on for some days, and finally interest began to pick up, and a few were saved. Then the pastor had to go to conference for a few days, but he left the meeting in the care of one or two good laymen, and upon his return the interest was still growing, and continued for six weeks, until ninety-six persons were converted, and united with the church. It was the privilege of the writer to hold a quarterly meeting in that church some time during the summer, and in the quarterly love feast, men and women shouted the praises of God. It was the warmest place spiritually the writer had been in for some years.

"Old Salem" is still working for God, and His cause, all because of the faithful prayer of one faithful soul who has since gone to his reward.

A. B. C.

Gracious Revival Follows United Prayer for Names on Lists.

In the town of Illinois, some twenty-five years ago, I was pastor of the Congregational Church. There had been no revival of religion in the community for some years. The church buildings were in bad repair, and many of the young folks were growing up without any real religious experience. I mean, without a change of heart. A real revival was greatly needed. Some of the members of the church were burdened for the salvation of the young people, while others were little concerned. The first thing that we attempted to do was to renovate the run-down buildings, this helped to prepare the way for the next thing that was upon my heart, the salvation of the young people.

I made known the burden of my heart to some of the members of the church, and requested them to write the names of unsaved persons upon slips of paper. When these lists were handed in we found from one to ten names on the different slips. Over fifty names were sent in to the minister's desk within ten days. We then, all agreed to pray for the salvation of those on our list, we did so for weeks.

After thirty days we decided to begin a series of revival meetings. Ten days before the series of meetings the praying members of the church met each night, for united prayer, remembering the entire list. Nightly evangelistic services followed. One week was about ended, with no apparent results. At the end of seven days, one Saturday night, the house was well filled, and there was a stillness at the close of the meeting. The benediction was pronounced, but to my surprise only a few left the church, of about three hundred people. A number resumed their seats, and as I went down the middle aisle I found a number sobbing I knew at once that conviction had seized the people, and that the revival was on.

It was after twelve o'clock when we dismissed the meeting. Men went from that service under deep conviction of sin. A lady of the community sent for me early next morning, saying that she thought her husband had lost his mind, as he had spent all night in the barn, praying. But when I reached the home I discovered that she was mistaken, that he had only lost his sins, and he was happy and in his right mind. On Sunday night we could not close our meeting until after one a. m. Scores were saved, and on the following Sunday we received thirty-two young people on confession. Sixteen of these were young men. Others went into the Methodist Church, and some came to us later in the year.

Five years ago I visited my old parish, and found many of these converts now the pillars of the church. God answers the united petitions of His people for the unsaved, when they exercise faith. "If two of you shall agree on earth as touching any thing that they shall ask, it shall be done for them of my Father which is in heaven" (Matt. 18:19).

N. McQ.

The Chill of Respectability Prayed Away.

I was holding meetings in Ohio. It was with a single church, and in a University town. Because of its aristocracy, university, and somewhat unique history the town was coated over with self-righteousness and a deadening respectability. The people were exceedingly conservative, and what was taught in the schools was adverse to the Word of God and to prayer. The pastor of the church, however, was a man of God and a thorough believer in the old Book. For weeks he and many of his noble people had been praying for a revival.

At the time of which I speak, I had been preaching nearly two weeks. There seemed to be no signs of an awakening. The people came, listened attentively, and just as before, went away without much prayer, and without ringing testimonies. I seemed to be preaching against a cold barrier back from which my voice rang in mocking echoes. Our efforts seemed a flat failure. The self-satisfied people went on in their indifferent ways, while many of the university students scorned the emphasis laid by the evangelist upon the power of the Gospel and the efficacy of prayer.

Well, we were at the end of our own dependence. We fell prone upon God's precious promises and appointed a day of prayer. To the joy of our hearts, the people came and went all through the day. Fasting was a natural part. The people forgot to be hungry. The soul had meat to eat of which the multitude knew not. "Heaven came down our souls to greet, and glory crowned the mercy-seat." We repeated God's promises. We asked in His name. We forsook our sins. We confessed our sins one to another. Victory was given unto us by the Lord.

Toward the evening hour a hush fell upon us. We were upon our knees, but in silence. Tears of repentance fell from the eyes of God's people. The Holy Spirit came upon us in power. That evening we expected a great breaking down of stubborn wills, and a glorious beginning of a mighty revival! But when the icy breath of the faithless and scoffing ones swept the audience, it sent a chill through us again. The expected power did not fall! We must be tried further. God had heard. The assurance had been given, but the blessing was withheld.

The next evening an after-meeting was announced in the room below the auditorium. To reach it everybody had to pass the outside door. Some feared all would go out and to their homes as before. But, no, the Spirit of the Lord directed our footsteps. The large room was crowded to the doors. The people were crying unto God now. Hearts were tender. Conviction was pungent. The singing was of the Spirit. A few audible prayers were offered. A brief word spoken by the evangelist, and the invitation extended to publicly confess Jesus Christ as Lord and Saviour. The silence was oppressive, then broken by a sob. Soon two sisters came forward, then two more, and a new Pentecost was on!

Within less than two weeks fifty-two twice-born men and women entered the church by baptism, and the community was shaken by a most glorious manifestation of divine power. It was the day of prayer that opened the flood-gates of power upon God's waiting children! H. W. J.

It is a serious thing to pray! We may be taken at our word.—*Moody.*

An Apparently Fruitless Ministry Blessed.

I had been preaching for a half dozen years but my ministry was not blessed with revivals. This was not because I did not yearn for the salvation of souls, and not because I did not preach the very truth of God, but there was a lack somewhere, which was remedied by the visit of a friend.

This friend was singularly honored of God in winning souls. He preached in my church for a week and I was disappointed that no one came forward within that period. However, while staying in my home, he talked of nothing but revivals and the salvation of souls. It seemed to be his meat and drink, and while no one was led to take a stand for Christ I found stirring within me a new passion for the lost.

My friend left me on Friday evening and I had to prepare for the services of the Lord's Day. My work at that time was on a circuit of country churches, and involved a drive of twenty-five miles on Sunday before reaching the church where revival services were being held. As I thought over the subjects upon which I should speak, God laid on my heart a burden for a young woman who lived in my neighborhood. I was really surprised at this, because the young woman in question rarely ever came to church. There was a stigma upon her birth, and although she had a name in the neighborhood for high moral character, she seemed to avoid public assemblies. Humanly speaking, it was a most improbable thing that she would be present at the revival services, and indeed I had never entertained a hope of reaching her, yet the Spirit of God kept stirring within me prayers for her salvation.

On the Lord's Day, as I drove around my circuit, this same spirit of intercession was upon me, and as I drew near the church in the evening I felt confident that the young woman in question would be present and that God would speak to her through the message. After kneeling in the pulpit, in prayer, I arose and was greatly rejoiced to find her sitting in a pew at the very front of the church. After the service, I said just a word or two to her and, immediately, the fountains of her heart were broken up and she expressed a great longing to become a follower of Jesus Christ, but went on to say that she felt she could not take a public stand for Him.

I left this young woman with God and continued to pray for her. On Tuesday night of the same week she came back to the church with another young woman, and as soon as the invitation was given, came and kneeled at the altar, bringing her friend with her.

Best of all, the Lord continued the spirit of intercession in my own heart and, although the village had not been visited by a revival for years, the work which began with this trophy of grace went on until seventy had sought and found the Lord.

The young woman in question became at once a worker in the church and one of the most useful factors in the community. Several years afterwards, a devoted Christian young man of that little church married her, and their home has become a center of light and blessing.

The lesson of trust in God which I learned on that occasion has followed me through the years. The church to which I was appointed shortly after this experience, had a congregation of well-to-do, self-satisfied people, who not only had had no revivals for years, but did not seem to desire them. I had learned, however, that if one soul is taken upon the heart of a Christian worker and made a subject for earnest prayer, God will begin to work, not only in that soul but in others. I found my faith confirmed, for in the month of August, when from a human point of view revival services were out of the question, God graciously visited His people and a number were saved. Year after year this experience was repeated in the same community, and young people enmeshed in worldliness were brought into the kingdom of God, in spite of the lack of sympathy on the part of their parents, and even against their parents' opposition.

L. W. G.

Faith puts God between us and circumstances.—*Webster.*

The Lord teaches His people to expect and pray for what He soon means to work.—*McCheyne.*

CHAPTER VII.
PRAYER FOR VARIOUS OBJECTS.

Deliverance from Temptation.

I consider prayer talking *with* the Lord rather than *to* Him. I was converted at the age of seventeen, and when teaching school at the age of twenty-one, a base temptation,—"a thorn in the flesh,"—assailed me, one which I had boasted previously as being freed of. Becoming spiritually proud the Lord had left me to myself on that point and the temptation threatened to overwhelm me. I prayed day after day for deliverance, yet the battle continued; the enemy did not break through, however. After long conflict on my knees the Lord revealed that I had been self-reliant, spiritually proud, and after confessing my sin I told Him I despaired in self and He spoke to my inner consciousness, "Reckon yourself to be dead indeed unto sin, but alive unto God, through Jesus Christ our Lord." My whole being confidently replied, and not alone my lips, that I would thereafter reckon thus. Calm and confidence were mine that moment and I went forth knowing I was delivered. That verse has been one of my mottos from the Lord for over forty years and the deliverance has been abiding.

H. T. C.

Lights for Gospel Boat Offered Before Prayer for Them Was Expressed in Words.

Dr. R. A. Torrey, when superintendent of the Bible Institute at Chicago, sent a number of us students on a Gospel boat down the Illinois River. The entrance was poor and had no light. As I was uptown in the place where we had landed, the dealer I was talking with said, "Brothers, I was at your meeting last night and I noticed at the entrance it was hard to enter, being so dark. I have a two-light coal-oil chandelier here. I will gladly fix it up and give it to you, if you will accept it." I said, "Indeed, I will; it is very kind of you," and went with the lamps to the boat. I went through the hall where meetings were held in the boat, and as I opened the door to the sleeping rooms in the rear, there were the boys on their knees, and Brother Cotton, who is now somewhere in England, was praying and asking God to send them a light for the entrance. The prayer was answered before it was offered, for there I was with a fine two-light chandelier (one light would have done), with founts and all complete.

F. H. B.

Vile Theatre Closed and Re-opened as Gospel Hall.

I was converted at Charleston, S. C., my home, August 13, 1900, after living a life of the worst kind of debauchery for twenty-five years. In this city was a variety theatre, known as the "Star Theatre," one of the lowest dens of vice that was ever open for variety shows. Here prize-fighting was held nightly, and lewd women held full sway. It was also the headquarters of safe-blowers, a gang of thieves that went over the state and then came to Charleston to spend their ill-gained money in this theatre on lewd women, whiskey and "dope," and having a fast time in general. This was during the early part of 1904.

I began to pray God to close up this vile place, and to drive the devil out, for he surely was getting his work in upon the young men of that and other cities. Within three months my prayer was answered. The mayor of the city gave the proprietor of the theatre notice to close up, "stock, lock and barrel," and to get out.

The dear Lord then placed it upon my heart to re-open the place for religious services. This I did, and on the 24th day of April, 1904, the place was dedicated for this purpose, and it has been under the Holy Spirit's control ever since. Thousands of people have been in the building, and have heard the sweet message of Jesus and His love. Today hundreds are preaching the Gospel of Jesus Christ all over this land of ours, that were converted to Christ through this work.

O. D.

Suitable Lodgings Secured.

Just before returning to college one fall, I was in greatly impaired health and dreaded going back lest I might not be able to stand the strain of study. I dreaded, too, being away from home. The load of foreboding fear was almost intolerable.

On the way I had occasion to change cars, with an hour or more between trains, and while waiting, walked a short distance from the depot, reading my little Testament as I walked—the last few verses of the sixth of Matthew. With all the earnestness of my heart I asked God to direct me to a quiet room in that college town and to provide for me in every way. Suddenly the awful load lifted, and I returned to the depot *perfectly at peace*.

A train was pulling in which had passed through the college town to which I was going. I stepped up to a man who alighted and whom I had never seen before and asked him if he knew anyone in the town. "Yes," said he, "I live there myself." My next question was whether he knew of any quiet rooms there for rent. "Yes, I have one in my home, and I'll go right back with you myself, and if it isn't what you want you'll be under no obligations." He had not expected to go back on that train, but he went anyhow, without any word or suggestion from me.

His home was in the *quietest* part of town, *just* the right distance from the college buildings, and the room *exactly* suited both me and my pocketbook, and was cozy and comfortable in every way. It was God's immediate answer to the agonizing cry of my heart.

A. N.

God Greater Than Circumstances; Water-Motor Shut Off.

My wife and I had been away from home all the week and came home very tired on Saturday evening. We hurried through the choir practice (she was organist and I was director) and went home and to bed. I could not get to sleep. I was so deeply impressed with the fact that I had neglected to have the usual season of prayer with a very devout young man who was a member of the choir. I was obliged to get up, dress and wade in deep snow for half a mile. I found the young man crouching in the rear of a store and greatly depressed. He had asked God especially that he might have prayer with me that night and his faith was being shaken by the fact that I had hurried home. We went to the warm church without speaking. Usually we prayed in a small room through which we passed; but we chose, not knowing why, to go into the main audience room and to lay our faces on the pulpit platform.

During his prayer I heard a slight click in the great organ and knew then that my wife had neglected to turn it off after the choir meeting. I knew, too, that there was no other place in the building where I would have heard that little sound. On account of peculiar conditions in that organ, had it been left running, the belt would have run off the water-motor before morning and the organ been greatly damaged.

I turned off the water, finished the season of prayer and went home. As I entered our room my wife awakened and asked me if I had turned off the organ. It seems that very soon after I left the house she remembered that she had failed to turn it off. She could not get into the church as I had the key. She simply asked God to attend to it and went to sleep.

L. S. C.

Bread When Bread Was Needed.

We were on the frontier in mission work, located in a small town of about 1,200 people and seventeen saloons. A Roman

Catholic priest visited the place once a month; that was the only church work aside from our own. We had made a rule not to buy anything unless we had the money at hand to pay for it.

One summer there was visiting us a lady friend and her daughter from Milwaukee, and at the same time some very dear friends of ours (a Presbyterian pastor and his wife). During the visit of these friends our money gave out entirely (this was no new experience); our larder, however, was in fairly good shape with the exception of flour. We had no flour and no money to buy with. We had made a rule not to tell anyone our *personal* needs with the exception of our heavenly Father. We had bread for breakfast, but there was none for dinner. Wife and I had privately talked over this lack, and it was taken to God in prayer. The forenoon wore away with no bread in sight, and no money and no flour. Things were cooked, the table set, and the noon-hour arrived, but no sight of a supply of bread. I cannot say that there was no anxiety on the part of myself and wife. We should have had perfect confidence in our heavenly Father, but the flesh was a bit anxious.

We were all ready to set down to the table, simply waiting for the boys to return from school. Watching for them from the window I saw the oldest boy coming with a bundle in his arms. I immediately stepped to the door and as soon as he was within calling distance I called: "What have you in that big bundle?" He replied: "Mrs —— called me in and said, 'Arthur, I wish you would take this bread to your mother. I don't know what possessed me, but when I was setting bread I made a mistake somehow, and made a double batch. I guess your mother will know what to do with this.'"

It is needless to say that we had plenty of bread for dinner that day. We are sure that the heavenly Father caused the good woman to make the extra amount, without her knowing why it was.

J. O. B.

A Sewing Machine Provided.

While at the Moody Bible Institute as a student I worked for my meals in a private boarding house near by with several other boys. We served as waiters and soon came to know the people whom we served. At the same time I was doing some photographic work to help along with expenses.

One morning after breakfast I was showing one of the men some photographs I had taken a short while before. He asked me if I would not take some for him and a date was set to take the pictures. They turned out fine; in fact, he liked them so well he ordered another lot, paying for the first ones finished. When I brought him the second lot he astonished me by saying: "Now, I can't pay you for these pictures, for we have to move and I need all the money I have. But my wife has a sewing machine that she has been using, which is really worth more than what I owe you, but if I were to sell it I probably wouldn't get as much, so if you want it on my account you can have it."

Well, I thought, a sewing machine is better than nothing, so I guessed I had better take it. But what to do with it was the question. A sewing machine was about the last thing on earth I needed. But as I passed into the kitchen one of the maids was talking to another about renting a sewing machine. I spoke up, and said: "What will one cost you, Miss Lita?" "About two dollars a month," she answered. "Well, I have one I will let you have for half of that, if you want it." The arrangement was made and one of the boys helped me move it to her room.

Several months passed by and I soon received in rental the amount of the original account. I still had the machine on my hands. The maid needed it no longer. Then again arose the question, "What shall I do with it?" Then the thought came, "Give it to some poor needy family; there are hundreds who need it." It seemed so direct I could but answer, "All right, Lord, but who? Show me who."

Some days later one of the married students came to my

room on an errand. As he was about to leave instantly the suggestion came, "Give the machine to him, he is the one." I asked him to come up to the room the next day and in the meantime took the matter to the Lord once more. The longer I prayed the more I was convinced that he was the one to whom I should give the machine. When he came up the next day I said: "A—, I have a story to tell you," and I told him the incident of the machine as I have told it here, adding, "I don't know anything about it, but the Lord has laid it upon my heart to give it to you and it is yours; go and get it."

Ere I finished tears were running down his cheeks and this is what he told me: "Mr. Z—, we need a sewing machine in our home more than anything else. We are poor, working and struggling our way through school. We did not know where it was to come from, so we took the matter directly to the Lord and there has not been a day in the last weeks that we have not asked Him to send it to us. He has heard our prayer."

J. E. Z.

A Railroad Man, a Young Convert, Gets Help in Special Need.

I belonged to a secret order that gave suppers and dances. That was all right until I was converted, and then I did not like to dance very well. But they would have them anyhow, and the next morning after a big time, fellows would meet me on the street and say, "I saw by the paper that you had a big dance last night." My answer would be, "No, not I. I had nothing to do with it."

On one occasion the question of a supper and dance came up, and I did my best to vote it down, but I could not. Then I said to them: "Now please remember I can not have anything to do with this thing, good, bad or indifferent. Can not have anything to do with it." But in due time six tickets came to my house from the home of a church member, a friend of mine, five to sell and one to buy. I took them back to the home and told the people that I could not handle those tickets. They insisted that it was my duty for the benefit of the treasury of the order, and that if I did not want to go to the dance I ought to sell the tickets anyhow. My answer was: "I can not sell tickets to those same people that I am preaching salvation to." They got real angry at me.

Going home I cried because I had lost a friend. I was just a young Christian, and I had to be true, but now I had lost a friend and a church member too. I knew nothing yet of my Bible only that I loved it. Every day it was being made more precious to me. I did not know where to turn or where to look, but I said to the Lord, "I want you to show me what to do." I had never been told to go to the Bible for such things, but since that night I have read in John 16:13: "When the Spirit of truth is come, he will guide you into all truth." So He was guiding Jim that night, the babe that I was. When I got home I picked up my Bible that I had just bought, and it fell open to the third chapter of 2 Thessalonians, and there I read:

"Now we command you, brethren, in the name of our Lord Jesus Christ, that ye withdraw yourselves from every brother that walketh disorderly, and not after the tradition which he received of us. * * * And if any man obey not our word by this epistle, note that man, and have no company with him, that he may be ashamed. Yet count him not as an enemy, but admonish him as a brother."

Now, I want to ask you if He did not answer my prayer? I want to ask you if He could have done a better job if He had been in my room in the flesh and had His hand on my shoulder and looking me right straight in the face? I turned around to my desk and wrote out a withdrawal card. They told me I would be sorry, but I have never been sorry.

J. B.

Definiteness of aim in prayer, combined with a holy persistency will surely hit the mark.—From *"Billy Bray."*

An Obstinate Watch Made to Go.

I had been conducting union Bible classes in Ontario that winter and making my home at London. The Y. M. C. A. at St. Thomas asked me to address their men's meeting one Sunday afternoon, and I planned to take the last train out Saturday evening on the Michigan Central. For some weeks my watch had been out of repair, and not being able to have the work done, I had purchased a cheap Ingersoll watch; but even that would not go. As a result, I missed the train. Upon inquiry, however, I found that there was possibly a delayed train on another road. I hurried over to the other depot and fortunately caught that train.

It was a stormy night and I sat in the car seat, quite cast down in spirits. Taking the Ingersoll watch out of my pocket, I realized that I had missed the train for lack of a suitable timepiece, and wished I had one. Something seemed to say, "Why not ask the Lord to make it go?" But, I thought, the Lord is not making watches go. Then came the verse: "If you abide in me, and my words abide in you, ye shall ask what ye will, and it shall be done unto you" (John 15:7). So far as I knew I was abiding in Him, and His Word abiding in me. Again the suggestion came, Ask the Lord to make it go, but I refused for quite a while, feeling that it would be foolish to do so. But over and over came the prompting and the promise.

Finally, I bowed my head and said, "Lord, make this watch to go." I gave it a shake and placed it to my ear. It was running! I had done this many times before but to no avail. It continued to keep time as long as I needed it. So real was the experience and the consciousness of God's presence, and so definite was the answer to prayer, that I wrote on the margin of my Bible the day and the hour, with these words opposite John 15:7, "This includes watches."

N. H. C.

"If ye shall ask any thing in my name, I will do it" (John 14:14).

Boards Lake Michigan Steamer That Had Already Departed.

I had just closed an evangelistic meeting in the central part of Wisconsin, and was hurrying to Milwaukee to catch the evening boat for Chicago, in order that I might spend the Fourth of July with my boys. Our train was late and I saw that I was liable to miss the connection. I definitely prayed that God would hold the boat and enable me to meet it. As soon as the train stopped, I was off and caught the first street-car to the docks. As I reached the wharf, I found the boat swinging out into the river. I called to the captain and asked if there was any way to get on. He replied, no, that I would have to go to Racine (by rail, about twenty-five miles south, where the boat also landed). I stood there for a moment, with bowed head, looking to my Father for the answer to the prayer on the train, considerably tested in faith but not wavering. Suddenly the captain shouted out, "Go down the bank of the river and we will pick you up!" I began to praise God for answer to prayer, and moved in the direction indicated. Just as I started, a young man came rushing down to the dock, and seeing the boat out in the river, he began to swear. I gently rebuked him, and said: "Just a moment my friend; God is answering prayer and stopping this boat so as to take me on, and you can get on too, if you will come this way." After they pulled us both on board, the young man turned to me and said: "Do you mean to say that God stopped this boat in answer to prayer?" "Yes," said I, "that is exactly what He has done." "Well," he said, "there must be something in it," and he showed me a letter he had received from some Christian woman who had written to him while he was in prison. He had just been discharged after serving a five years' sentence. Needless to say, we had an earnest talk of the One who is able to save and keep from sin.

N. H. C.

If we lived nearer heaven we should have earlier notice of God's purposes.—*Moody.*

CHAPTER VIII.

PRAYER IN RELATION TO MISSIONS AND MISSIONARIES.

Old Strength Restored.

For a whole year my health was so poor that I feared I must give up the work falling to my lot as a missionary's wife (in China), and go to a sanatorium for treatment. Consumption, asthma and chronic sore throat all seemed to threaten me. These added to chronic rheumatism made life a trial; for I must get about, as there was no one to take my place. The household must be attended to, sick people treated, the women's meetings kept up, and visitors received. Seeing that it was the Lord Himself that had put me into the work, I felt bold to cry unto Him for help, and to ask the prayers of God's people. The Lord blessed the treatment given by a kind medical missionary, and gradually the discomfort lessened, and the old strength returned. Now I am able to continue in the work and find daily strength given.

X.

Ulcerated Mouth Healed.

Last year when at an out-station, a child was brought to me with a fearfully ulcerated mouth, black inside, loosened teeth, and every symptom of what is stated in the medical books to be a most fatal disease. She was an outsider, and I am not a trained medical worker, and I knew if I attempted the drastic treatment prescribed, her mother would not bring her again. All I could do was to cleanse it and give her a wash to use at home. The Chinese said the child would die, and I thought so.

That night the little one was much on my heart, as I thought of her suffering and slowly dying in the comfortless surroundings of a Chinese sick-bed, and I prayed very much for her.

Next day when she came I heard exclamations, and, behold, her mouth was half well! The black had all disappeared; the swelling had gone, the child was well on the way to recovery and quite healthy looking. She steadily got well, and stronger in every way, and my prayer now is that in some future day the incident may lead to spiritual results in her home.

M. E. C.

A Bale of Silk Recovered.

Amongst the members of a congregation centered at a China Inland Mission Station there is a devout man, who has a silk shop in the city of Nanking. At the time of the rebellion just two years ago he had ordered a valuable bale of silk, which had been delivered at his place of business in the city, when hostilities broke out. The Christian, who was himself at Laian, was at once told by his neighbors that he was sure to lose the silk, when the city was looted. He, however, who had been praying much about it, had the assurance that the Lord would preserve it, and, notwithstanding appearances to the contrary, he held steadfastly to this belief during the succeeding weeks. When it became possible for him to go down to Nanking, he found the store in which his silk had been placed had been looted. Part of a wall had, however, fallen exactly where his bale had been placed; hence, it had escaped the observation of the soldiers, and was found in safety—a true and striking answer to prayer, even though the matter itself was not of great material importance.

C. B.

Delivered from Brigands.

Our mission station (China) is situated in the country, at the foot of a range of hills. The nearest Mandarin walled city which governs our district is thirteen miles distant. So that in unrestful times like the present we are without the slightest protection. Our mission station is within gunshot of the village, whose inhabitants are now well armed against the brigands, who make incessant raids on the villages around, burning and torturing the people to extort money. During the year and a half we have worked here our village has been attacked five times, yet latterly with poor success. From the first our only resource was prayer. Arms of any kind we had none, but we had the unfailing promise of God our Saviour, "Lo I am with you *alway*"—the missionary's fortification against the enemy. God's promises in these times of alarm and danger have been most sweet, and numberless times the shaking nerves have been quieted and the palpitating heart eased. Not once have we been touched, though during the first raid, while one of the business houses was in flames and yells rent the air, the brigands passed right by our gateless cart-gate, firing off a revolver as they passed by. These deliverances have made a great impression upon the heathen and in a remarkable manner have paved the way for the preaching of the Gospel.

X.

An "Ancestral Hall" Becomes a "Gospel Hall."

We had lived in our own hired house, next door to a large Ancestral Hall, for two full years. Next year our lease would expire and we must renew it, for—oh, ten years perhaps. So we thought and planned, when, lo! notice was served upon us to quit.

Oh no! impossible! We would give more rent, we would take a long lease, twenty years if necessary, but we *could not* leave; we had only just settled in, and the women's work was growing both in the city and in the country districts round. So we pleaded, but this moved the landlord not at all. He wished to live in his own house; the foreigner must go.

We cried to the Lord in our trouble, and this is how the answer came:

One day a "little bird" whispered that the Ancestral Hall next door might be for sale, and, impossible though this seemed, the rumor persisted. True we had often turned longing eyes to that high, splendid building, and had coveted it for a Gospel Hall, but as a center for women's work only, such a thought would scarcely suggest itself. Still we remembered the Word had said, "I * * * will do better unto you than at your beginnings." And, as an encouragement, one skillful in these matters came five days' journey to see if he could help us; if purchase was possible. He made preliminary inquiries, then came to us and said, "No, the thing is impossible. You will never succeed in securing this property," and departed.

We again went to the Lord and said, "Lord, we know that the things which are impossible with men are possible with Thee; *if this would be for Thy glory,* grant that the joint owners may be willing to sell, and the money be provided *soon,* before the hot weather comes; if not, we do not want to touch this thing. "Show us Thy will, Lord."

Walking by, a day or two later, and standing a moment to look up at the hall, a voice said, very distinctly, "It is yours."

Two or three days passed, when a representative from each of the clans came to say they were willing to sell. A dear fellow worker said, "The money is ready," and so, quickly, before the end of the following week, the deeds were written, the ancestral tablets taken away and burned. No more would incense be lit and prayer be made to these, but instead would rise daily the sacrifice of praise and thanksgiving to Him who alone is worthy.

Saved from Flood on a Queensland Sheep Run.

The following is from memory of what my sister wrote of herself, husband, and two little girls being saved from flood in the beginning of this year, 1917. Her name is Mrs. H. C. Seton, "Makonda," near Clermont, Queensland. She wrote with a stump of lead pencil on the pages of a small note book found at the woolshed where they took refuge when the water abated.

My very dear Mother:

We are all here alive and well and write to relieve your anxiety about us and to tell you that we are sure we are saved in answer to your prayers. The flood came upon us unexpectedly and has been the highest ever known.

We thought we should be safe in the ceiling of our house which we reached, as the waters crept up and over each of our previous places of refuge. But it soon began to look as though this place too would fail to shelter us and we prayed to be guided as to the next move. My husband tore a batten from the ceiling and put it across from the roof to the fork of a young tree to form a bridge, and this offered a very faint hope of escape. Helen went across first bravely and steadily over the raging, roaring torrent without a flinch or a murmur. I went next; then we persuaded little May to follow but had to take time and patience to encourage the little thing to venture over as I held my arms out to her in front and her father helped her from behind. At last we got her across and none too soon as the house was lurching so that the plank was only just long enough to span the distance and a minute or two later would have dropped. Bert just managed to get across on it and drew it into the tree. This tree was new growth from an old root; the old trunk having been cut down near the ground.

It was remarkable that there were just three new young stems from this old root, and each stem had a branch which formed a fork above the flood waters and pretty nearly at the same height. Bert put the batten from one fork to another to form a seat for us and he stood in the third fork. And here we spent the long hours of waiting and watching in the storm of wind and rain with the roaring torrents rushing beneath us. It seemed impossible that the young tender wood of the new growth would stand the tremendous strain of the heavy wind and water, and we felt that any moment we might be swept away. We knew that God was our only deliverer and our hearts here kept lifted to Him.

As the dawn began to glimmer, imagine our joy, mingled with doubt, as we fancied we could see familiar objects emerging above the top of the water. And the eagerness with which we watched for clearer light. As the light came we saw that the water had fallen many feet and was rapidly subsiding. Not a vestige of our house was left, but our hearts were overflowing with praise and thanksgiving that we were all spared and had received no harm.

F. E. McC.

Prayer for Special Form of Service Answered.

In 1899 I returned from China badly broken in health, after only two and one-half years in that country, where I expected to spend my life in missionary service. As the trouble was a nervous one it did not seem likely that I should ever be able to return to China, which was heart-breaking and meant a re-arrangement of life's plans. After two months in the delightful climate of Southern California I was able to take outdoor employment during forenoons by which I earned sufficient to pay board and room. The afternoons and evenings were spent in different phases of city mission work.

During my school days and while in China I had had the very happy experience of giving two-tenths of my income back to the Lord's treasury; but after returning from China I was so poor it was only by strictest economy that I could return to the Lord His tithe. I had *loved* to give and knew many places where even small sums would accomplish much for Christ.

One afternoon, some months after I had taken the secular employment, I was in my room praying for a blessing upon the small sum which I was able that day to put by for the Lord out of one month's earnings. As I prayed there leaped from my heart an unpremeditated prayer, that if I could not myself be a missionary nor earn much with which to help missionaries, God would entrust the money of other people with me for missions. I was surprised, but felt quite sure that the prayer had been indited by the Holy Spirit, who knows the mind of God and what He is willing to bestow, and with all the faith I could muster I said "Amen" to the petition, and trusted God.

I went about my work, and in just a few days received from a high-school teacher in an adjoining city a check for $150, with the request that I should use it for missions wherever I thought best. And since that day there has passed through my hands $484,776 for the Lord's work and workers in different mission lands. Most of this money has come from those who knew me, but no inconsiderable amount has been received from people who never saw me. Many letters have been received from missionaries, telling that the gift sent reached them just at a time of need, and it has been remarkable how often the amount sent has been just the amount they needed.

The writer can lay no claim to merit or worth in connection with this answer to prayer, because he did not even desire or ask the gift until suddenly prompted to do so by the indwelling Spirit. R. D. S.

Deliverance from Impending Flood.

Before I went to the city of Changteh, in Honan, there had been two occasions when the Lord wonderfully delivered the property of the China Inland Mission from fire by turning the direction of the wind at the critical moment. Another fire occurred in 1908 which was so threatening that an iron trunk was got ready to put the Mission registers and account books into. In this case also God answered prayer and the fire was stayed.

But the special incident that I wish to recall and put down for the glory of God, is one of deliverance from great flood. It was the summer before the first revolution (1911) when I was stationed at Nanchow, 100 miles from Changteh. I was visiting at Changteh, and my departure was delayed for a week by the sudden rise of the Yuen river and the closing of the city gates to keep out the water. When at last I got away, I had a depressing journey through a wide spread flooded area. On my arrival at Nanchow, my colleague, Mr. Draffin, told me the following striking incident.

Unlike most cities, Nanchow has no wall, and when the water of the river rose and kept on rising, so proportionately did the fears of the magistrate and his people. This official had caused a live dog and pig to be thrown into the waters to appease the god of the river, but the sacrifice was without avail. Next an idol from one of the temples was carried out and set up on the bank of the river. The official addressed the senseless image thus, "If you stop this flood and so save the city, we will build a suitable structure over you here, where you will be worshipped in gratitude; but if you don't, or can't, well then you will be washed away." Still the waters surged on, a stream about half a mile wide rising with fearful stubbornness and seeming to play with the topmost ridge of the embankment as though to add to the suspense and fear of the people.

In their extremity and despair some of the men stopped Mr. Draffin on the street with the startling request: "Oh foreign teacher, won't you pray for us to your God?" "Yes," was his prompt reply, and straightway he gathered some of the church members at the church. Knowing what was intended many of the people crowded in to watch and listen. They saw a few of their fellow townsmen on their knees and heard definite, simple, direct supplication to the great God to cause the flood to abate. "Now we will go and see the answer," said those that had prayed. This they verily did and they found that the water had receded an inch or two. The climax was passed and the water continued to fall. A calamity to the city and district had been averted.

Those who saw God's marked answer to prayer were greatly impressed and God was glorified in that heathen community.

J. G.

Answers to Prayer in the China Inland Mission.

PREPARED BY F. A. S.

A Father's Anger Cooled.

At the China Inland Mission Conference at Niagara in 1917, Mrs. W. H. of Kiangsi told the following two incidents:

A man was bitterly angry because his young daughter and daughter-in-law used to come into the Gospel hall next door and read the Bible and believed in Jesus. This he regarded as a disgrace. One day he beat his daughter dreadfully, and he locked them both up in a room and gave them opium to kill them, for he said he would rather kill them than have them join the Jesus religion.

Much prayer was made for them always, and on this night the missionaries spent much of the night in prayer. The next morning the father went to the room and found them, not only not dead, but quite well. He gave up his active opposition and sometime later he invited the missionaries to take dinner at his house and did them the honor of himself cooking the meal.

"But prayer was made continually."

Delivered from a Riot.

On one occasion, just seven years from the day when they were first rioted and driven out of Kanchow Fu, when all their property was destroyed or stolen, they were threatened with serious riot in another city. The magistrate and literati had hired a number of rough characters to do the mischief.

One day was beautifully bright and clear. They went to bed after much prayer, knowing that the attack was set for the next morning. When they arose a deluge of rain was falling, not in drops but in sheets. It rained steadily all day, and not even a dog was on the streets. The next day was again bright and clear. The superstitious people said, "You see even heaven does not sanction our driving them out," and the plan was dropped.

"But prayer was made continually."

Praying for Rain.

The small city of Pingi, on the borders of Yunnan and Kweichau, in West China, had resident missionaries for several years. Later Mr. and Mrs. Hanna left the place in charge of native workers and went to another city about seven days' journey further west. In 1914 Mrs. Hanna felt led to visit the old station to give help and encouragement to the Chinese workers. When she reached the little city—which the writer remembers as being situated on the banks of a small river, with orange orchards near by and snow-capped hills overlooking it—she found the people in a ferment of excitement and distress. The rain had failed to come when it was needed, and it seemed that the crops would be a failure and local famine and suffering must result.

A few days later a crowd of distressed people gathered at the *yamen* (magistracy) and demanded that, as the "father and mother of the people," the magistrate should go to the temple and pray to the gods for rain. He replied that the people in many parts of China had forsaken their idols and broken them to pieces without suffering for it, that the idols were the work of men's hands and could neither help nor harm them, that he could not worship them, but if the people wished he would go to the "Jesus" hall and ask the Christians to join him in prayer to their God. This was accepted, for something must be tried, and anything would do that brought rain. Accordingly, this non-Christian official came, with his wife—who had been brought up in a Christian school—to the Mission Chapel and sought the prayers of God's people.

It was a keen test of faith, but the Christians responded to Mrs. Hanna's leading and earnest prayer was made. In His tender care God saw fit to answer at once, for whilst they were still on their knees rain began to fall. The next day it rained more heavily, and the crops were saved. The mandarin's wife said she would come regularly, and she offered to play the "baby" organ at the services. The sequel in blessing upon God's work in that city yet remains to be recorded.

JAMES TAYLOR'S PRAYER.

About 1880 the writer met in the London Home of the China Inland Mission an old man named James Taylor. Fifty years before this man had been moved by the woes and the spiritual darkness of the Chinese people to desire that he might labor among them with the gospel. This being impossible, he prayed very definitely that God would bless his home with a son who should become, in his place, a messenger of light to those who sat in such gloom in China. God answered his prayer by giving a son, but his weak health all through boyhood made the fulfillment of the second part of the prayer seem impossible. Yet, in God's good time, the lad was strengthened, converted, consecrated, prepared, set on fire and sent forth to China, and, though never strong in body, James Hudson Taylor was enabled to support great and continuous labors together with no small hardships and trials for more than fifty years for the land of God's call.

The young missionary was not influenced towards China by his parents' direct guidance or suggestion. It was not until he had been in soul-winning and medical work for years in China that he returned to his Yorkshire home and heard for the first time the story of his father's early longing and specific prayer.

The story of Hudson Taylor's conversion is a record of pre-

vailing prayer. Born on purpose—as we may believe—for God's plans in China's evangelization, and in answer to his father's prayer, he was nevertheless a natural child who needed regenerating grace. At the age of fifteen he had turned to skeptical companions who made light of the Bible. His mother and his younger sister were much concerned for his soul's state.

One day the mother was visiting relatives some eighty miles distant, and, excusing herself after dinner, she went to her room, locked the door, and turned to God in prayer for her son, with the purpose that she would not go out to meet people again until she got the answer to her prayer. Here was the daring of a mother's great necessity and of a Christian's faith in God's purpose to answer prayer. Hour after hour did that mother pray, and as she prayed on God's Spirit was working in the lad's heart through the words, "It is finished," in a booklet that he had carelessly picked up. The mother's prayer was stopped, as if by a touch from God, and her lips were filled with glad praise instead, for the Spirit assured her that her boy was saved. It was even so, for he had come to realize that no effort of his was needed to complete Christ's payment of his debt, and that all he had to do was to fall down before God, accept His wonderful gift and praise Him for it. Thus mother and son were joined in Spirit at God's throne though far separated in the flesh. Two weeks later, when she came home, he tried to tell her the good news, but she stopped him and said that, though no one had written to her, she had been rejoicing for a fortnight over the good, good news, which God had spoken to her soul.

Lives Saved from Shipwreck and Valued Papers Restored.

In the early spring of 1903 we bade goodbye at Shanghai to W. B. S., J. D. N. and H. W. F., who had been visiting China in the interests of the China Inland Mission. They sailed on the P. & O. steamer "Sobraon."

The steamer had scarcely been from port twelve hours before telegrams told us that she had been wrecked on Tung-yung

Shan, a rocky islet off the China coast. Later messages brought word that no lives had been lost, but that the passengers' baggage had been stolen by piratical fishermen whose boats were hired to take the goods to Foochow. Clothing and bedding were quickly gathered, packed and sent off by a relief steamer. Earnest prayer for the safety of the travelers had already been made, and we gratefully recognized God's answer in preserving life.

Continued prayer was offered for their safe rescue from the island, and that no ill effects might be felt from the exposure and the rain which had fallen. J. D. N. wrote a note to the present writer, on the back of an envelope, in which he praised God for His safe-keeping, and that through it all their hearts had been preserved in peace and even joy in the prospect of going in quickly—though by a violent death—"to see the King." Referring again to a quotation well known among his dear friends, which was the Revised Version of the last verse of the twenty-third Psalm, he said, "It is true still that 'Only goodness and mercy shall follow me all the days of my life.'"

When told that all their property had been stolen, Mr. F. felt comparatively little regret for most of his goods—needful as they were—but he did most earnestly long and pray for the recovery of his notes of Bible readings, which represented half a life-time of prayerful study. This seemed almost beyond hoping for, as weeks went by and the chequered voyage, continued in different vessels, came at last to a close at London.

One day, J. D. N. said that he had received a notice from the steamship company that the battered remnants of their goods, which had been rejected by the pirates, had been discovered in another bay of the same island and had been brought to London, and asking the passengers to go down to the docks and identify them. Mr. F. could not go down at the time, so J. D. N. went alone, and found that almost everything was utterly spoiled by rough handling and salt water. Kicking a manila envelope with his foot, he discovered that it contained some of these very Bible studies by his friend. He searched further and found the whole six envelopes containing studies upon different general subjects. One envelope had evidently been torn and its contents scattered over the beach, for the sheets of paper were stained by mud and water. But it was evident that the Chinese who collected the things had been careful to gather up every piece of paper and put it back in the envelope. There was not one study missing from this series of readings on the person and work of the Holy Spirit, or any of the other subjects! Nothing else was recovered of Mr. F.'s belongings, except one old collar.

Faith was greatly strengthened and praise called forth by this specific answer to His servant's cry of need. It should be added that these strange writings which the Chinese fishermen-robbers had no use for, but which they were restrained from destroying, are being used of God to this day as the basis of most helpful teaching for the people of God.

A Converted Soothsayer Proves God.

One very interesting case in a village eight miles from Kaoping, China, is that of a fortune-teller. He has heard a little for some years. He and his wife both smoked opium. He reads well, and studied the New Testament. There he found that God would answer prayer, and save people from their sins. He determined to break off opium by prayer; they had no money to buy medicines, and though he suffered much, he got rid of the habit entirely.

Later he induced his wife to do the same, praying with and encouraging her, till she also won the victory. Then his mind became troubled about his fortune-telling, for he felt he could not be a Christian and continue to deceive and terrify people. He made his living chiefly by telling poor, ignorant mothers that their precious baby boys were under a malignant spell, which would destroy them, but that he would save them, if they paid him well and obeyed his instructions, which most were eager to do.

He spoke to his wife, but she discouraged him, saying: "We are poor enough now, but if you give this up we shall have nothing." He said: "God says he will give us what we need, if we seek righteousness, and this fortune-telling is unrighteousness. I ought not to do it." But she could not trust, and her lack of faith hindered him. Towards the close of the year he felt that he *must* give it up. She said: "What shall we do for New Year's?" He replied: "God will provide." For many days nothing came in, and they were living from hand to mouth till their last cash was gone.

Then, in the last days of the year, a man who wanted some important papers written, called him in, and he did the work so well that he handed him 2,000 cash (about 85 cents), sufficient to buy what they would need for the New Year holidays, lasting about two weeks, when no busines is done. He went home joyfully, saying: "See what God has given us. Shall we not trust him fully?" But the 2,000 cash were soon spent, the food eaten, and again want stared them in the face. "Go, and tell some fortunes, and buy us some food," said she. But he answered: "The God who provided for us at New Year's will not forsake us, if we are faithful to Him." "If I could see two pints of grain in the pot, I would trust Him, but the pot is *empty,* and we have nothing." "Will you really trust Him, if He puts two pints of grain in the pot?" "Yes, but where is the grain to come from?" "I do not know, but God does."

They went to bed hungry that night, but he still prayed and trusted. Next morning they were surprised by a call from an old friend living miles away, whom they had not seen for years. There was a native doctor of some repute, living in the village, and the friend had brought his sick boy to be treated. "Can you take us in for a day or two, old friend?" "How *can* we?" the wife whispered. "We have no food for ourselves and certainly none to offer them." "God will provide," answered the husband. "Come in, friend, and welcome!" The visitor turned to his cart, carried the sick boy in, laid him down, returned to the cart, and brought in a large basket of flour and a big bag of grain." "You will cook for us and for yourselves, please." The husband looked at his wife, but said nothing.

For three days they shared the visitors' food, till the sick boy had improved so much that they prepared to return home, taking medicine to complete the cure. The cart was brought to the door, the boy stepped into it, and the father followed. The host lifted the basket of flour, now half full, and the bag, which still contained more than a peck of grain, to place them on the cart. "Keep them, old friend; they are not worth the trouble of taking back; we have plenty more at home. And many thanks for your kind hospitality." The visitors left. *"Now* will you trust God, wife?" "I will, indeed, and serve Him, too. I'll unbind my feet at once." She did so, and came with her husband to the Christian services.

He is working hard at any kind of honest labor, including field work for a Christian farmer. Everywhere he testifies to what God has done for him.

F. M. R.

The Foreign Doctor Jesus.

The wayside messages of the traveling missionary in China are left behind, in spoken words or in the printed form, with earnest prayer that God will make the seed to grow. Thus was a copy of Luke's Gospel left with a restaurant-keeper after Mr. D. and Mr. F. had rested and taken tea in his place.

Soon afterward a Chinese doctor strolled in to drink a cup of tea, and, seeing the book, he picked it up and began to read about Jesus rebuking a fever, healing the sick and raising the dead to life again. He said to the owner, "Are you sure the red-haired foreigners left this? It tells about one Jesus who must have been a doctor, but I never heard of a doctor who could do such things as this man did." "Yes," said his friend, "the red-haired men have been round here all day preaching, and they live in the town thirty miles away." "Then," replied the doctor, "I'm going there to inquire more clearly about this foreign doctor, Jesus."

Not long after, this man came to the Gospel Hall and, on meeting Mr. F., he produced from his little bundle this same copy of Luke's Gospel, and said: "I want to know if these stories about Jesus are true. I'm a pretty good doctor myself, but I can't do anything like this, and I never heard of anyone else who could." Then the missionary sat down and patiently taught a willing listener of God's salvation through faith in Jesus. At that very first interview the doctor, whose name was Leh Tung-chen, gave his heart to Christ, taking Him as his own Saviour.

At once he began witnessing for his Lord in his native village and district. He often visited Mr. F. at Tientai, and he loved to sit in the street chapel and read aloud to the crowd which gathered around. He had been a Confucian reader whom the crowds listened to, and now he used his gift in reading and explaining the Scriptures. He met with contumely and hatred from his fellow villagers, and for Christ's sake bore it patiently.

Fire Stayed.

In the interior of China there is no provision for fighting fire, and so when fire begins they call upon their idols and often carry them out of the temples into the street and pray to them for help in full sight of the fire. It was thus when a fire occurred in the doctor's native village. The houses were burning and the people were clamoring and knocking their heads before their idols, but it was all in vain. The work of destruction went on, and the wind was blowing the flames in the direction of Dr. Leh's house.

Following the old custom in regard to public prayer in time of great calamity, the Christian came out of his house and knelt down before the excited crowd and prayed to God to deliver and protect him and his house. Some of the men trod upon and kicked him brutally, saying, "What are you doing there? We have cried to our gods and if they can't help us, do you suppose that the foreigner's God can do anything to save us?" But God did hear and answer, and vindicated His name in that heathen village. Whilst Leh was praying, the seemingly impossible happened and a sudden change of the wind turned the flames aside, when they had almost reached his house. To this day the house stands, with only a few small buildings around it, whilst otherwise the village is largely a pile of ruins.

The attitude of the people toward their Christian neighbour was completely changed, and although they did not accept the Gospel they respected and treated him kindly. A Christian church was gathered in the district, but located in another village, and there about thirty believers meet for worship, the result of this man's faithfulness, and that in turn resulted from a printed gospel, left behind with prayer.

After seven years of bright testimony for his Lord, the old doctor "went in to see the King," and his happy death sealed the witness of his consistent life.

This incident was told recently by Mr. F. at the China Inland Mission prayer-meeting in Toronto.

Day of Special Need.

We had special need for money one day and had been praying definitely for between one and two hundred dollars. The mail had come in, and there was no answer in it. I was perplexed and troubled, and being in charge at the time, I felt the burden of responsibility.

Not long after the mail was opened, a lady from a city 40 miles away came in, and I was called to see her. Two of her sons were in China, and the work of the gospel in that land of great need lay near to her heart. After some talk, our friend opened her little old-fashioned hand-basket and produced a thick roll of bills. As she handed them to me, she explained that a relative across the seas had died, leaving her a legacy, and this was a part of the money which she had been led to give to the China Inland Mission. She had evidently been impressed to take the train and bring us the money on this particular morning.

As in the case of the coal merchant (page 125), we would give no hint beforehand that might prompt a gift, but the gift having been made, we thought it our duty to give this friend the joy of knowing how God had led her to answer our prayers. The amount was a little more than the exact sum we had prayed for.

A Coal Merchant Made a Discovery.

At another time we were without money to purchase coal. It was winter and there was only furnace coal enough to last a few hours and we also needed coal for cooking. At morning prayers we prayed for coal for the day, on the principle of "Give us this day our daily bread." Another member of the household saw further and remembered that the coal merchants do not deliver less than a ton of coal. Thus, in view of the need for fuel, he prayed that God would send on quickly two tons of coal. I remember feeling that this was too specific a prayer, but evidently the Lord did not think so.

As we rose from our knees the bell rang and a friend entered. He was a coal merchant, the one from whom we always purchased. After inquiries about the families and the work, our friend said: "Mr. F., I was looking over our books yesterday and I found that my bookkeeper has been charging you the full retail price for coal, whereas I intended you to have a discount of fifty cents per ton. I found that I could not correct it without altering a great many figures, and so I told him to settle it by putting down to your credit two tons of coal, and you can have it sent up at any time." Mr. F. and I laughed outright, but it was a laugh that was akin to tears, a laugh of joy and praise to God.

Our friend was deeply moved when we told him the circumstances, and he shared our joy that he—deeply engrossed as he was in business—was still susceptible to God's touch upon his heartstrings, and that he had been led to come in on that particular day with that particular answer to prayer.

It is utterly impossible for faith to overdraw its account in God's bank. God could no more disappoint faith than He could deny Himself. He can never say to faith, "You have miscalculated; you take too lofty,—too bold a stand; go lower down, and lessen your expectations."—*C. H. M.*

SUBJECT INDEX

I. PRAYER FOR THE RECOVERY OF THE SICK

Page

Accident Injury, Prayer for Son 12
Baby's Life Spared............. 15
Bronchitis, Chronic, Child's Deliverance 21
Death, Given Up to, Recovers.. 11
Hearing Restored 12
Infant's Life Snatched from Death 17
Internal, Incurable Disorder Healed 12
Invalid Ten Years, Restored... 15
Lunacy Cured 11
Nerve Force and Strength Fail, Receives Renewed Energy.... 16
Operation Averted 18

Page

Operation Necessary, Submits with Peaceful Trust......... 20
Operation Successful, Prayer Offered 500 Miles Distant Answered 13
Optic Nerves Restored........ 13
Painful Affliction, Healed...... 14
Pneumonia, Deliverance from.. 17
Sick Child Recovers, Father Impressed, Later Accepts Christ 22
Typhoid Fever, Child's Prayer Effectual 16
Typhoid Fever, Recovery from. 19

II. PRAYER FOR FINANCIAL AID

Bible School Course Completed, Financial Aid Rendered..... 25
Bills Amounting to $100 Paid.. 32
Church Needs New Building, Funds Provided 26
Church Receives One Thousand Dollars Prayed for.......... 28
College President Proves God.. 37
Debt Lifted 26
Exact Sum Prayed for Received 27
Faith Mission Conducted and Supported 33
Financial Need Supplied by God 41
Flour Provided when Needed.. 35

Grief, Financial Aid in Day of. 34
Home Necessities Provided.... 25
Missionary Candidates' Temporal Needs Supplied.......... 39
Missionary Receives Money.... 24
Missions, Money Provided for.. 28
Pastor's Need Supplied........ 29
Provision for Unpaid Taxes... 36
Railroad Fare Received in Time of Need 24
School Days, Financial Crisis Removed During 31
Winter's Blasts, Protection from 30

III. PRAYER FOR DELIVERANCE IN TIME OF DANGER

Fire Approaches, But God Intervenes 43
Lost in Canadian Bush; Delivered 46
Mine (Coal) Explosion and Deliverance of Miners.......... 48

Railroad Engineer Saved in Wreck 45
School Boy's Experience....... 43
Sinking Steamer in Mid-Atlantic, Deliverance from........ 51

IV. PRAYER FOR GUIDANCE

Boy in Trouble Delivered...... 57
Brethren in Need Interviewed. 55
Change of Field Indicated..... 58
Christian Service, Led into and Equipped for 54
Christian Work, Guidance into. 63
Conflicting Prayers and the Results 66
Dream Used for Blessing...... 62

Education Provided in Accordance with James 1:5........ 56
Employment Secured 59
Field of Labor, Direction to... 61
Guidance in Choice Between Home and School Duties.... 70
Journey of 2,000 Miles, Leading in 54
Journey of 100 Miles Undertaken Without Visible Means. 69

126

Subject Index 127

	Page		Page
Ministerial Call Confirmed.....	55	School Children Subdued.......	57
Money Lost, But Bills All Paid in Short Time...............	68	Scripture Card in Office Window	64
		Sign Guides	59
Right Field Entered...........	65	Sorrow, Sustained in Hour of..	60

V. PRAYER FOR THE CONVERSION OF INDIVIDUALS

Apparently Fruitless Ministry Blessed 96
Athlete's Conversion 87
Banker Becomes a Christian... 78
Box Car, A Place of Conversion 74
Boy in Reform School Accepts Christ 82
Boy's Salvation and Education. 80
Brother Restored While on Trip 75
Daughter's Salvation 86
Drunkards, Cared for.......... 74
Enemies Reconciled 73
Father Converted 84
Husband Converted After Fifteen Years 76
Husband's Salvation 81
Infidel Father Believes........ 81
Mother's Prayer for Son...... 88

Notorious Character Saved..... 79
Politician Delivered and Made Whole 77
Prayer for Man Fifty Years, He Surrenders 74
Schoolmate Becomes a Christian 76
Sister and Family Converted.. 78
Sixty Years Old, Saved at..... 73
Son Prayed for Is Saved, Twenty-four Hours of Fasting.... 75
Sport Converted 85
Thirty-three Answers to Prayer During Series of Meetings... 83
Two Sons, Whereabouts Unknown, Accept Christ Day Request Was Made.......... 77
Wanderer Brought Home...... 79

VI. PRAYER FOR REVIVALS

Chill of Respectability Prayed Away 94
Church Members List Names, Pray, Revival Follows....... 93

Dead Town Revived 91
Fruitless Ministry Blessed..... 96
Results Increase Through Increased Prayer 91

VII. PRAYER FOR VARIOUS OBJECTS

Bread Provided When Needed.101
Deliverance from Temptation.. 98
Lights for Gospel Boat Offered Before Request Was Made.. 98
Obstinate Watch Made to Go..106
Sewing Machine Provided.....103
Steamer Boarded That Had Already Departed 107

Suitable Lodgings Secured....,100
Theatre Closed and Re-opened as Gospel Hall............... 99
Time of Special Need—Railroad Man—Young Convert Helped 104
Water-Motor Shut Off.........101

VIII. PRAYER IN RELATION TO MISSIONS AND MISSIONARIES

"Ancestral Hall" Becomes a "Gospel Hall" 110
Bale of Silk Recovered........109
China Inland Mission, Answers to Prayer in.................115
Deliverance from Flood........114
Delivered from Brigands.......109
Father's Anger Cooled.........115
Fire Stayed Through Prayer...123
Foreign Doctor,—Jesus 122
Life of J. Hudson Taylor, His Father's Prayer 117

Old Strength Restored.........108
Prayer for Special Form of Service Answered 112
Rain, Prayer for...............116
Saved from Flood on Queensland Sheep Run.............111
Saved from Shipwreck, Valued Papers Restored 118
Soothsayer Converted 120
Ulcerated Mouth Healed......108